eat · sleep · shop

STOCKHOLM

STYLE GUIDE

LISA ARNOLD

murdoch books

Sydney | London

CONTENTS

VÄLKOMMEN TILL STOCKHOLM!

For Swedes, subtlety and good style are not mutually exclusive. Take their wonderful concept of *lagom*, a word with no English-language equivalent, which has in recent years become something of a lifestyle trend worldwide. *Lagom* stands for the ideal balance: the optimal measure between too much and too little. In Stockholm, you will recognise *lagom* in the locals' fashion sense. People like to wear classic colours, such as black, white and navy, enhanced with well-considered details and jewellery in basic shapes. Swedish brands such as Filippa K, Hope and Acne Studios have given the world a minimalistic style that never goes out of date. Swedish brands have also long honoured a philosophy of sustainability; indeed, the Swedish climate demands durability of all products, from houses and cars to jackets and backpacks.

The Nordic light is something special. Even though each and every place in the world gets the same number of light hours in a year, they are distributed very differently. The further north you go, the longer the summer days and winter nights become. Under these extreme conditions – with up to 24 hours of light and darkness – it is no surprise that Swedes have developed a special relationship with light. They master lighting indoors and outdoors, design wonderful lamps and decorate coffee tables and pedestrian areas with candles. That's why Stockholm is a year-round destination: while summer brings outdoor cafés, boat tours and long walks in the sun, winter has its own charm thanks to the millions of lights in the windows and street, and a cosy atmosphere. And no matter the season: don't leave without initiating yourself in the Swedish tradition of *fika*, a slow-paced coffee break with a cinnamon bun and a friend.

Stockholm is also a great place to dive into Nordic design. When the lack of light and temperatures below zero force people indoors, the home becomes not only a place to sleep and cook, but a haven for days and nights, worth spending time and money on to make it beautiful, functional and inviting. And you don't need an invitation to a private dinner party to enjoy Swedish interior design, because more and more eateries take pride in being a *kvarterskrog*, a restaurant with a relaxed, living-room atmosphere where you can hang out with friends. Hotels, bars and even the smallest cafés are also thoughtfully furnished and stylishly decorated, forming an effortless beauty where everything seems to find its natural place.

Stockholm is a celebration of Swedishness, not only in the world of shopping and dining, but also outdoors. This capital is unlike any other because it comprises one-third water, one-third parks and gardens, and only one-third city architecture. Nature is a high priority for Swedes, even for city dwellers. Cycling to work, enjoying lunch in the park and paddling into the sunset are every-day activities for Stockholmers. As soon as the first rays of spring sun shine through, you'll find people sipping coffee outside, wrapped in blankets. Their love for *friluftsliv*, the outdoor life, is symbolised by the protected national park in the middle of the city center. The island of Djurgården is known for its museums, as well as for its former

Royal hunting grounds with oak trees as old as 400 years.

Being outdoors also means discovering Swedish architecture. Since Stockholm is built on islands, the different districts have preserved their individual characters. The cobbled streets of the medieval centre Gamla Stan are lined with historic houses in bold shades of orange, red and yellow. In elegant Östermalm, you will see richly decorated city palaces built by noblemen and wealthy industrialists. The modern Norrmalm, also called City, is full of glass office blocks and boasts Europe's first skyscrapers. Thanks to the hills and waterfronts, there are plenty of scenic walks, as well as restaurants with outdoor seating boasting panoramic views. And don't miss the chance to travel by boat, be it a short ferry ride or an extended archipelago tour.

After years of living in Stockholm, the city never seizes to amaze me with its stunning landscape and its impeccable style. I am delighted to share my favourite places to visit with design fans all over the world. Let this book be your guide to unique places to eat, shop and stay – so that you can discover the true sense of Swedish style and how it can make your life easier and more beautiful.

Welcome to Stockholm:
Välkommen till Stockholm!

A DAY IN STOCKHOLM

For me, a good day starts with a healthy breakfast, and that's why I head to **Broms** (p. 94) for sustenance. I cross Narvavägen street to get to the water, wander along Strandvägen boulevard and take in the view of the boats. There's no way I can walk past the design furniture in **Svenskt Tenn** (p. 76) or **Malmstenbutiken** (p. 80) without a good browse.

Next, I head over to Norrmalmstorg square, where I bring myself up to speed with the latest fashion trends at **Filippa K** (p. 39) and **Acne Studios** (p. 33). It's very handy that the Stockholm fashion district starts here, and so I stroll further along Biblioteksgatan to the **MOOD** shopping mall (p. 35) and the upmarket department store **NK** (p. 46).

I cross Kungsträdgården park and the bridge with the golden crown to get to the island of Skeppsholmen, home to the **Moderna Museet** (p. 198) and **Ark Des**, the Swedish Centre for Architecture and Design (p. 203). Both of these house inspiring collections, and entry is free. For lunch, I stop at the restaurant in the Modern Art Museum, which has lovely water views.

Refreshed, I take the ferry to Slussen and walk up the hill to SoFo via Katarinavägen street. In SoFo, I browse the many small, independent stores, among them **Grandpa** (p. 145), **Marimekko** (p. 113) and **Tambur** (p. 128).

Götgatan Street takes me back in a northerly direction. I meander through the laneways of the old city centre and take a detour to the factory outlet of **Swedish Hasbeens**. Continuing on my bargain hunt, I follow Drottninggatan street all the way across Norrmalm to find the inconspicuous factory outlets of **Whyred** und **Rodebjer** at the end of the pedestrian mall.

All this shopping calls for a break before heading out again for the evening. I stay at the **Hotel With Urban Deli** (p. 22) because it is centrally located and I can enjoy my aperitif on the roof terrace.

Reinvigorated, I walk over to **Knut Restaurang** (p. 216) and treat myself to a dinner of a Norrland plate, an elk burger and cloudberries with vanilla ice cream. Then I take a taxi to **Mälarpaviljongen** (p. 241) and finish my day listening to lounge music at the pontoon bar.

The Hornstull markets are a favourite among trendsetters.

STOCKHOLM TIPS

THE CITY'S HISTORY

Stockholm is built across 14 islands and has 57 bridges. The city, which is currently home to about 950,000 people in the metropolitan area and about 2.3 million people in the greater Stockholm area – a full fifth of the total Swedish population – was founded on the island of Gamla Stan or Stadsholmen (Island of the City) in 1250. Gamla Stan is at the confluence of the eastern arm of Lake Mälaren and the Baltic, and fresh and salt water meet at the Slussen locks. People only started to settle on the islands and promontories around the city centre in the 17th century, when the old town was becoming too crowded and dirty.

The names of many of Stockholm's suburbs indicate their location relative to the old town: Norrmalm is literally the northern, Östermalm the eastern and Södermalm the southern settlement, while Kungsholmen, which was originally called Västermalm, lies to the west. Until 1810, the external borders of all these parts of Stockholm had customs offices (*tullar*), which collected duties on goods brought into the city. While these offices have long been abolished, they are still reflected in place names such as Hornstull, Skanstull and Norrtull, and Stockholmers looking for a central place to live will often say they want somewhere 'within the tullar'.

If you are curious to find out more about Stockholm's history, both the Medieval Museum (Medeltidsmuseet, *www.medeltidsmuseetstockholm.se*) and the City Museum (Stadsmuseet, *www.stadsmuseet.stock holm.se*), which reopened in 2019 after renovations, are highly recommended.

OUT AND ABOUT

Stockholm's public transport system comprises three metro lines (*tunnelbana* or *T-bana*), buses and (a few) trams. If you stay in a hotel along the green metro line, you'll reach most of the major attractions without needing to change. With its 100 creatively designed stations, the Stockholm metro system has been dubbed the world's longest art gallery, and Kungsträdgården station is particularly well worth visiting.

Ferries are also part of the city's public transport network. Ferry line 82 (Djurgårdsfärjan) connects Gamla Stan/Slussen with Skeppsholmen and Djurgården, while line 85 does its rounds between Stadshuset/Klara Mälarstrand, Södermalm/Söder Mälarstrand and Kungsholmen/Kungsholmstorg. SL passes and smartcards can be used for all modes of public transport.

Stockholm is very bike-friendly, and an extensive, well-established network of CityBike stations (*www.citybikes.se*) offers great flexibility.

BEST TIME TO VISIT

As Stockholm is a long way north (900 km north of London) its climate is cool with very distinct seasons and a long, dark winter. However, as the city is on the sea, its temperatures are milder than you might think. Winter temperatures rarely drop below -10°C (14°F), summer weeks can be quite warm, reaching up to 30°C (84°F), and the sun shines more often than in other parts of the country.

The best time to visit Stockholm is between May and August. Locals leave the city from early July to mid-August to relax at their summer cabins, allowing visitors to hunt for bargains during the end-of-season sales. This might sweeten the fact that some shops and restaurants also close for the holiday season.

If you come in the middle of summer, this is a great time for combining a city trip with a more extensive holiday in Sweden. The country has plenty of swimming spots and hikes for exploring its beautiful scenery. Sweden grants people the so-called 'freedom to roam', which allows anybody to camp in nature, to fish and to pick berries and mushrooms.

OPENING HOURS

Most shops are open daily, with the exception of major public holidays. In fact, shopping and browsing are favourite Sunday pastimes for many Stockholmers. Supermarkets are also open daily, generally between 8 am and 9 pm.

A CASHLESS SOCIETY

These days, hardly anybody in Stockholm still carries hard krona; people instead pay for everything by card, from small items such as postcards to major purchases such as hotels. Many shops, restaurants and museums no longer even accept cash. Paying by credit card is standard, and you'll need to enter your PIN number. Debit cards also work in most cases.

EATING

Swedish gastronomy is consistently of very high quality, from corner bistros to Michelin-starred restaurants, but it comes at a price. For dinner, you should expect to spend at least 300 krona per person for a main course and drink – with plenty of room for spending more if you go for two or more courses.

Daily lunch menus (*dagens lunch*) are an inexpensive alternative for gourmet travellers: On weekdays, many restaurants, including quite a few high-end ones, serve lunch comprising a main dish, bread, salad, a soft drink and coffee for 100–150 krona. Tips are not necessarily expected when dining out for lunch or dinner, as restaurant staff are paid well. However, feel free to reward good service with a few extra krona (5 per cent is enough).

NIGHTLIFE

Some Stockholm clubs and bars have fairly strict bouncers who may not only check your ID, but also your outfit. Stockholmers put effort into how they look and like to dress up for going out. If you don't want to feel out of place, a shirt and black trousers or a dress are recommended for women, and men should also wear shirts. Wednesday nights are 'Saturday's little brother', when many locals head out to their favourite pubs. Bars close at 1 am every night, but nightclubs really only start happening at about midnight on Fridays and Saturdays and keep going until 3 am.

ATTRACTIONS

With interactive museums, exciting art collections and elegant palaces, Stockholm is a great year-round destination for culture buffs. Many of the city's major attractions, including the Vasa Museum and Skansen, are located closely together on the island of Djurgården. If you're considering the Stockholm Pass: don't, it's really not worth it. We recommend you visit the destinations of your choice at your leisure instead of committing to an intense sightseeing tour by buying this expensive pass. Twelve outstanding museums, among them Moderna Museet (p. 201), ArkDes (p. 203) and Hallwylska (p. 24), are free anyway.

ACTIVITIES ON THE WATER

If you want to see Stockholm at its best, it's really worth spending as much time as possible on and along the water. The Strömma shipping company offers city and dinner cruises with fantastic views, the latter also with excellent food (*www.stromma.se*).

For something more active, try a pedal boat (*www.sjocafeet.se*) or a guided kayak tour (*www.stockholmadventures.com*), which is also suited for people with no kayaking experience.

ARCHIPELAGO ADVENTURES

Sandhamn can be reached by either of two ferries: Strömma's Cinderella line departing from Strandvägen (two or three times daily, depending on the season) or the Waxholmsbolaget line (various daily departures from Stavsnäs, which can be reached by bus No. 433 or 434 from Slussen, *www.waxholmsbolaget.se*).

While the cheaper, but less romantic, route from Stavsnäs is popular among locals, the Cinderella boats mainly take tourists to the Stockholm archipelago, departing from the city centre and stopping at the picturesque islands of Vaxholm, Grinda and Gällnö en route to Sandhamn. A trip to the archipelago requires a little preparation. Plan your departure and return times in advance, as the ferries don't run frequently. If you intend to stay overnight on one island and maybe hop on to another on the following day, make sure you book ahead. The number of hotels and hostels in these idyllic locations is limited, and they are very much in demand during the short season (June to late August) by both tourists and locals.

OUTLET SHOPPING

Swedish design is pricey, but luckily you'll find not only flagship stores of renowned brands in the city, but also well-stocked factory outlets offering pieces from past collections at half price.

A Rodebjer Revisited
(outlet, see map pp. 16–17)

B Whyred Selection
(outlet, see map pp. 16–17)

C Mini Rodini Treasures
(outlet, see map p. 148)

D Swedish Hasbeens
(outlet, see map p. 180)

E Acne Archive
(outlet, see map pp. 208–09)

With is famous golden crown, Skeppsholmsbron bridge is one of Stockholm's most picturesque spots.

Big city life! Kungsgatan was modelled after the streets of Manhattan.

WHERE TRENDS ARE BORN
NORRMALM

Stockholm's inner city is where you go to feel the pulse of the Swedish design scene. This densely built-up suburb was comprehensively redeveloped in the modernist style in the 1960s. However, you'll still come across traditional streets with picturesque city palaces and Europe's oldest skyscrapers in between glazed high-rise buildings and wide streets. Norrmalm's best addresses are taken up by stylish restaurants, leading hotels and flagship stores of renowned fashion labels. The area around Norrmalmstorg square and Biblioteksgatan street is Stockholm's fashion district. Local cafés, rooftop bars and parks offer a great escape from the bustle of the two main streets, Drottninggatan and Kungsgatan.

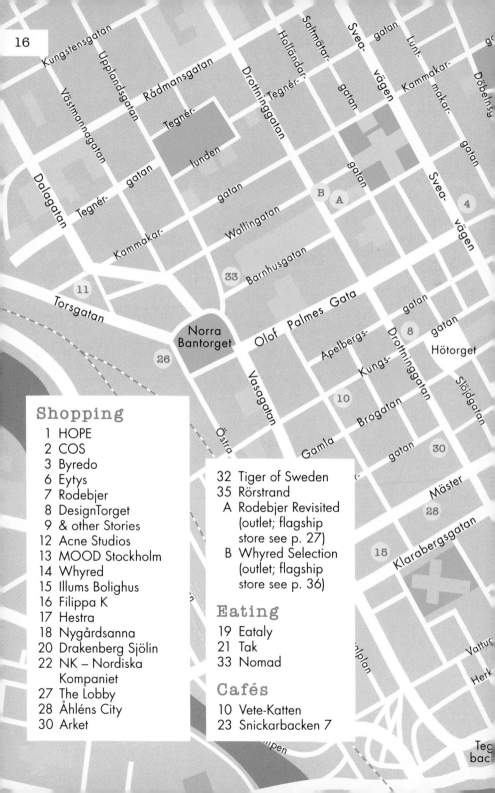

Shopping

1 HOPE
2 COS
3 Byredo
6 Eytys
7 Rodebjer
8 DesignTorget
9 & other Stories
12 Acne Studios
13 MOOD Stockholm
14 Whyred
15 Illums Bolighus
16 Filippa K
17 Hestra
18 Nygårdsanna
20 Drakenberg Sjölin
22 NK – Nordiska
    Kompaniet
27 The Lobby
28 Åhléns City
30 Arket

32 Tiger of Sweden
35 Rörstrand
A Rodebjer Revisited
    (outlet; flagship
    store see p. 27)
B Whyred Selection
    (outlet; flagship
    store see p. 36)

Eating

19 Eataly
21 Tak
33 Nomad

Cafés

10 Vete-Katten
23 Snickarbacken 7

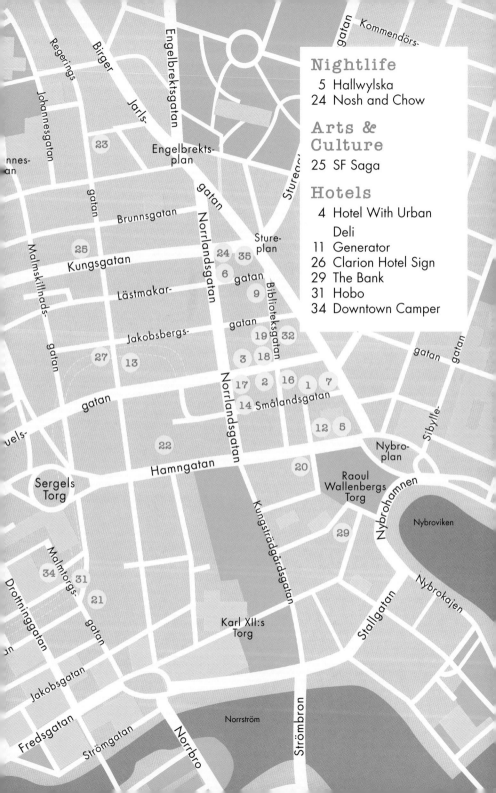

Nightlife
5 Hallwylska
24 Nosh and Chow

Arts &
Culture
25 SF Saga

Hotels
4 Hotel With Urban
    Deli
11 Generator
26 Clarion Hotel Sign
29 The Bank
31 Hobo
34 Downtown Camper

1 HOPE

This airy flagship store of leading Swedish brand HOPE is the place to go for immaculate women's and men's fashion. HOPE collections combine timeless pieces with original details, and the designers use prints sparingly. One of the brand's specialties are jackets. In 2017, they started to label each item with sizes for both women and men to invite customers to explore the full range – a statement that brings the very Swedish ideals of openness and equality into the realm of fashion.

Smålandsgatan 14
www.hope-sthlm.com

2 COS

Shirts a little too long, dresses a little too big, pants a little too short – COS plays with silhouettes that are just outside the usual. But the looks work because the collections stick to classic colours. Just one or two pieces, which easily combine with t-shirts or your favourite jeans, will revive your wardrobe with a fresh Nordic breeze. COS is the big sister of bargain label H&M, but works in high-quality fabrics and timeless designs to make its garments much more durable. COS does both women's and men's fashion.

Biblioteksgatan 3
www.cosstores.com

BYREDO

SEVEN VEILS

EAU DE PARFUM

3 Byredo

Byredo only launched its scents presented in minimalist bottles in 2007, but has already made its way into upmarket department stores in the US and Hong Kong. Its flagship store sells the full range, including scented candles and accessories as well as perfumes. The name is derived from the word 'redolence', meaning 'pleasant (often evocative) fragrance'. Byredo's founder Ben Gorham, a rather unconventional perfumer with tattoos and a former career as a basketballer, creates scents based on personal memories.
Mäster Samuelsgatan 10
www.byredo.se

4 Hotel With Urban Deli

A windowless hotel room? That's nothing
too unusual in Stockholm, partly because
land is at a premium in the city, and partly because it gets light at 3 am in summer, making it difficult for guests to sleep
in. This designer hotel features feel-good
underground caves with effect lighting,
sound insulation and comfortable beds
for a restful sleep. It also includes a popular restaurant, a hip supermarket and a
'roof park' with a bar and view of the
city, which is open throughout summer.
Sveavägen 44
www.hotelwith.se

5 Hallwylska

You'll find what is most likely Stockholm's most charming bar in the courtyard of a town palace built for the wealthy Hallwyl family in the late 19th century. From early May through to mid-September, Hallwylska serves drinks and bar food in a Mediterranean ambience created by olive trees, sculptures and a beautiful façade with balconies and columns. On Saturdays, brunch is served from 11:30 am. The palace is very well preserved and houses a museum that is definitely worth a visit.

Hamngatan 4
www.hallwylska.com

6 Eytys

Check out the shoes of fashion-forward Stockholmers, and you'll often find they're wearing Eytys sneakers. Eytys designs feature only sparse decorative elements and instead celebrate functionality and exciting materials on soles made for tough city streets. Yet – or perhaps as a result – this young label for casual unisex shoes (founded in 2013) has broken into the Paris fashion scene. The Stockholm store, the label's only branded one, stocks the current collection of light canvas sneakers through to chunky and even risqué, limited-edition designs.

Norrlandsgatan 22
www.eytys.com

7 Rodebjer

When Carin Rodebjer wore her hand-made designs on the streets of New York in 1999, so many people asked here where she'd found them that she turned her passion into what is now a highly successful women's fashion label. Soft silhouettes, playful prints and subdued colours give her designs an unmistakeably feminine touch. Rodebjer expresses the personality of women who aim for authenticity rather than perfection. Visit the Rodebjer Revisited outlet (Drottninggatan 92, see map pp. 16–17, A) for samples and pieces from past collections. Flagship store: Smålandsgatan 12
www.rodebjer.com

8 DesignTorget

Here's a store that demands a lot of restraint from fans of Nordic design – it's difficult not to go overboard. The 'Design Square' offers a wide range of contemporary, innovative items for stylish living and cooking, from jewellery and stationery through to toys and books. Check out its reinterpretations of old classics and technical innovations such as loudspeakers, headsets and the invisible bicycle helmet. This treasure chest of form and function stocks renowned brands next to one-off pieces by emerging designers.

Kungsgatan 52
www.designtorget.se

9 & Other Stories

This cool member of the H&M family sells young fashion that isn't quite as ephemeral as that of its better-known sibling. Cheerful colours, loose cuts and playful prints evoke a sense of holidays in the sun. The concept store has everything its (female) customers might want or need, from underwear, swimwear and skincare through to stationery. Its collections, which come from three design studios in Paris, Stockholm and Los Angeles, are all framed as part of stories.

Biblioteksgatan 11
www.stories.com

10 Vete-Katten

This large café, which extends across several rooms and a cosy courtyard, is a Stockholm institution. It was founded by Ester Nordhammer in 1928, at a time when women had just been given the vote and few of them started their own businesses. Ever since, this patisserie has been synonymous with delicious cinnamon scrolls, cakes and tartlets. Many Stockholmers shop here for special occasions or to sit in one of the charming 'parlour rooms'. The lovely courtyard (open in summer) lets people forget that they are in the middle of the city.

Kungsgatan 55
www.vetekatten.se

11 Generator

The globally popular Generator hostel chain finally opened a Stockholm branch in 2017. Located right between Norrmalm and Vasastan, only a few minutes' walk from the central railway and bus station, this is Stockholm's most convenient place to stay if you want something inexpensive and sociable. There are dorm rooms as well as single, double and family rooms, with or without private bathrooms. The contemporary room design combines comfort, functionality and security. A café and bar serve as meeting points.

Torsgatan 10
www.generatorhostels.com

12 Acne Studios

The cult label, founded in 1996, was and still is the trailblazer of Nordic minimalism in fashion. Its creations are usually characterised by clean understatement, but sometimes Acne designers like to mix in out-there prints, unusual fabrics or a nod or two to the 1980s. Acne ankle boots are long-standing classics on the streets of Stockholm. The flagship store and the upmarket department store NK in Norrmalm have the current collection, while the Acne Archive outlet in Vasastan (Torsgatan 53, see map pp. 208–9, E) sells older pieces at half price.

Flagship store: Norrmalmstorg 2
www.acnestudios.com

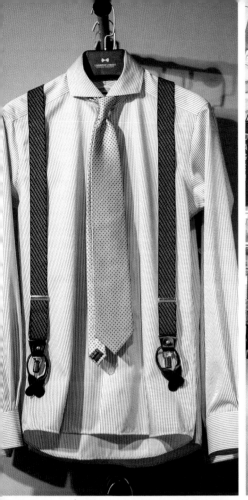

13 MOOD Stockholm

You'll find this unique shopping centre tucked away between high-rise buildings and office blocks. With a softly lit maze of shops, tiny relaxation gardens and a backdrop of lounge music, this couldn't be further from the neon-lit standard shopping fare. Three dozen stores, including J. Harvest & Frost, Svenssons i Lammhult, Rituals, Scotch & Soda and Hobbs, offer a wide range of fashion, accessories, cosmetics and furniture. If you get hungry, try the Asian eatery EAT, Pizzeria 1889 or an oversized cinnamon scroll at Café Egoiste.

Regeringsgatan 48
www.moodstockholm.se

14 Whyred

Whyred, one of Sweden's largest international fashion brands, has been renowned for its bright colours, classic cuts and durable fabrics since the late 1990s. Its creations are inspired by art and music, and its fans include pop stars such as Madonna, The Hives and Oasis. Norrmalm is home to not only the recently renovated flagship store but also the well-stocked outlet store Whyred Selection (Drottninggatan 94, see map pp. 16–17, B), where you'll find pieces from past collections at half price.
Flagship store: Smålandsgatan 10
www.whyred.com

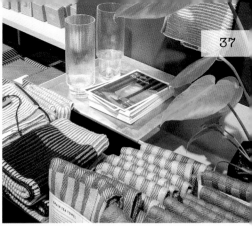

15 Illums Bolighus

A visit to the Stockholm branch of this Danish designer warehouse is a must for fans of innovative designs for stylish homes. Illums Bolighus has been an internationally recognised institution for cutting-edge furnishings and fashion for almost a century, so expect to be surprised. Whether you're after a vase, scented candle or pizza cutter, you're bound to find something to make your life more colourful or easier. The store also sells functional fashion by selected Danish designers to add a splash of colour to your wardrobe.

Klarabergsgatan 62
www.illumsbolighus.com

16 Filippa K

Filippa Knutsson's fashion credo is: 'Style means clothes that accentuate instead of drown out their wearer's personality. Fashion should be aesthetic, balanced and harmonious.' The label's flagship store showcases how this looks in practice. Knutsson's menswear and womenswear collections consist of minimalist, well-fitting, high-quality pieces in classic colours. Each item is an investment towards a stylish wardrobe for any occasion. BTW: there's a second-hand store specialising in Filippa K fashion on Södermalm (p. 154).

Biblioteksgatan 2
www.filippa-k.com

17 Hestra

This brand has been synonymous with dependable gloves for the chilly Scandinavian climate since 1936. It started out as a family business in Småland province, became a favourite among skiers in the 1960s and is now a label that sells over 400 styles to 25 countries. Its range extends from functional sports gloves through to elegant leather handwear. The Hestra flagship store is a great place to find a practical Swedish souvenir for winter. Stacked with stylish boxes, the rear of the store feels delightfully old-fashioned.

Norrlandsgatan 12
www.hestragloves.com

18 Nygårdsanna

Anna Bengtsson's store is a tiny spot of rural Sweden right here in the capital. Bengtsson, a designer from Dalarna province, has been sewing since she was nine. She then studied fashion in Stockholm and turned her final project into a successful brand. Nygårdsanna has stood for comfortably cut clothes made from sustainably produced fabrics, mostly in shades of blue and white, for about 25 years. The brand's motto is understatement that underlines the wearer's personality instead of overpowering it with extravagant cuts.

Mäster Samuelsgatan 6
www.nygardsanna.se

19 Eataly

This heavenly place for lovers of Italian food is located in a former cinema from the Golden Twenties, complete with chandeliers and painted ceilings. Come here for delicacies ranging from cheese, cured meats and pasta through to *dolci*, either to take away or dine in at the La Piazza restaurant. Eataly Stockholm defines itself as a cultural and culinary meeting point between north and south Europe, which fuses delicious sun-blessed foods with Swedish designer gastronomy. Why not put together a picnic basket of Italian specialties to enjoy alfresco?

Biblioteksgatan 5
www.eataly.se

20 Drakenberg Sjölin

The jewellery designed by Andrea Drakenberg and Ellen Sjölin hits the sweet spot between over- and understatement with small pieces of perfection. Their restrained designs with delicate chains and tiny pendants suit everybody. Bracelets, necklaces and earrings are accentuated with timeless elements such as pearls, asymmetrical leaves and knots. The brand's founders describe their collections as a mixture of raw elegance and sophisticated fragility. This also sums up their store: an exquisite haven in the midst of a bustling city.

Hamngatan 11
www.drakenbergsjolin.com

21 Tak

Right above the roofs of Norrmalm, raw-food queen Frida Ronge creates Japanese-inspired delicacies made from seasonal Nordic produce. Tak (meaning 'roof') comprises three restaurants: a bar serving dishes made of raw ingredients, a restaurant with hot and cold foods, and a bar for cocktails and light meals. There's also a roof terrace that's perfect for refreshing drinks in summer, mugs of something warm in winter and breathtaking city views all year round.

Brunkebergstorg 2–4
www.tak.se

22 NK - Nordiska Kompaniet

NK is to Stockholm what Harrods is to London or KaDeWe to Berlin. This Art Nouveau palace right in the city centre sells Nordic and international brands over six floors, including fashion, jewellery, accessories and furnishings, as well as delicious food. The stylish interior alone, with galleries surrounding a courtyard with a glass roof, is worth a visit. Of NK's eleven cafés and bistros, the best is Bobergs Matsal, where award-winning chef Björn Frantzén serves his signature dishes in an exclusive ambience.

Hamngatan 18–20
www.nk.se

23 Snickarbacken 7

These former 19th-century stables are now home to a cosy, candlelit concept café that serves snacks and light meals, such as cinnamon scrolls, sandwiches, salads and soups. The walls are hung with contemporary paintings and photographs, with exhibitions changing several times a year. At the back of the café there's a shop selling stylish objects, including Scandinavian-designed one-off ceramics, cushions and blankets, as well as homemade jam.

Snickarbacken 7
www.snickarbacken7.se

A selfie in Kungsträdgården park is a must when the cherry trees blossom in spring.

24 Nosh and Chow

This stylish restaurant, open since 2013, is also known as the Townhouse, and its broad gastronomic offerings indeed extend across several levels of a city palace built in the late 19th century. At its heart is a luxuriously styled contemporary BBQ restaurant on the ground floor, which has received a number of awards for its design. Here, the mouthwatering aroma of steaks cooked over hot coals wafts from the open kitchen. Upstairs, around the inner courtyard, you'll find Bernies & Mono nightclub and cocktail bar.

Norrlandsgatan 24
www.noshandchow.se

25 SF Saga

This movie theatre, which dates back to 1937 and was once the place for grand opening nights, has retained its glamorous interior from the heyday of Swedish cinema. The foyer features an impressive, curved staircase and beautiful lighting. Sweden, like many European countries, does not dub movies but instead shows them with subtitles so that fans of international cinema are able to enjoy the latest films without speaking a word of Swedish.

Kungsgatan 24
www.sf.se

26 Clarion Hotel Sign

Stockholm's largest hotel is also one of the city's design icons, with rooms and lounges furnished with classic Scandinavian design objects. Relax in chairs designed by Bruno Mathsson, Alvar Aalto or Arne Jacobsen and admire the glass decorations by Philippe Starck. On the rooftop, you'll find Spa Selma with a heated outdoor pool – a perfect place for enjoying the balmy, long summer evenings or relaxing in style in winter. The eighth floor also has a rooftop bar with breathtaking views.
Östra Järnvägsgatan 35
www.nordicchoicehotels.com

AHLVAR GALLERY
VOLVO
HORIZN STUDIOS

IN THE
MOOD FOR
SHOPPING

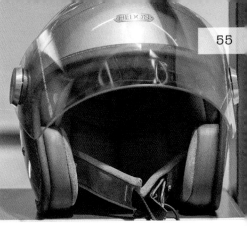

27 The Lobby

This urban marketplace for design, fashion, lifestyle and technology is in constant flux. Since it opened in 2018, quite a few labels have come and gone from its space – which is precisely the idea. The dynamic store extends across two levels. The ground floor is where you'll find established brands, while the lower floor is rented out on a monthly basis to emerging designers, who showcase their products in small pop-up shops. Depending on the day, you'll find just about anything here, from t-shirts to headphones and bags, even bridalwear and car brands.

Regeringsgatan 61
www.thelobbystockholm.se

28 Åhléns City

Visit Sweden's largest department store
for an insight into current trends in
affordable fashion, furniture and beauty
products. The store's range extends from
its inexpensive private label to known
Swedish and international brands such as
Esprit, Tommy Hilfiger and Ilse Jacobsen.
Its ten food outlets offer a variety of
sustenance to make your shopping trip
a true experience. Visit the roof terrace
of Pane Fresco to relax or Sally Voltaire
& Systrar for creative, healthy food.
Klarabergsgatan 50
www.ahlens.se

29 The Bank

This boutique hotel with 115 cosy yet elegant rooms opened in 2018. Situated in a magnificent palace that is a mixture of Renaissance and Art Nouveau architecture, both its name and many interior details reference the fact that the building was once a bank. The hotel restaurant is excellent, and guests can enjoy a picture-perfect view of Nybroviken bay, the harbour, Strandvägen boulevard and the green island of Djurgården from the balcony on the seventh floor.

Arsenalsgatan 6
bankhotel.se

30 Arket

Part of the H&M group, this cool fashion store, which opened in June 2018, sells more upmarket fashion. Its shelves are stocked with classic, mostly uni-colour and therefore easily combinable basics for women, men and children. The shop is generously laid out and also sells a wide range of cosmetics, homewear and books. Its café serves vegan and vegetarian snacks inspired by New Nordic cuisine.

Drottninggatan 53
www.arket.com

31 Hobo

Forget traditional hotel rooms with a bed, a chair and a wall-mounted TV. The hypermodern Hobo hotel experiments with strong colours, a lot of wood and unusual interior features: instead of a wardrobe to hang your clothes in, you'll find a perforated room divider. There are pot plants suspended from the ceiling, and you can enjoy a view of the city from your bed. With its fresh design and moderate prices, Hobo is a firm favourite among travellers. Its trendy bar is a great place for guests to finish the day with a cocktail or two.

Brunkebergstorg 4
www.hobo.se

32 Tiger of Sweden

Founded as a men's outfitter in 1903, Tiger of Sweden converted into a modern design label for classic men's and women's fashion in 1993. Its collection focuses on suits, shirts and dresses for everybody who wants to look and feel good at work or events, thanks to high-quality designs and fabrics. If you prefer a more relaxed style, choose from a wide range of denims, where you'll find the serious attitude of the more formal wear replaced by bold fringes, faded colours and styles from skinny to generous fits.

Biblioteksgatan 12
www.tigerofsweden.com

33 Nomad

This small restaurant with an open kitchen serves quintessentially Swedish, beautifully prepared cuisine at unbeatable prices. The menu only includes about seven or eight dishes at any time, which change weekly. Two standards are always available, though: the S.O.S. entrée of marinated herring three ways and *köttbullar* meatballs in a creamy sauce with lingonberries. The restaurant has a picturesque courtyard with regular live jazz and DJ sets. It is associated with the hostel next door.

Upplandsgatan 2

www.nomad.bar

34 Downtown Camper

This experimental hotel, part of the Scandic group, is on Brunkebergstorg square, which town planners recently rebranded as an urban hotspot after a century of neglect. This is the place to go for urban explorers who want an authentic Stockholm experience. There's a 'lifestyle concierge' who provides advice on a range of outdoor activities, and the hotel rents out kayaks. On the 9th floor, you'll find The Nest, a bar and spa complex with amazing views. It's also open to the public, although admission to the spa will set you back about 600 krona.
Brunkebergstorg 9
www.scandichotels.de

MONICA FÖRSTER

A designer with a passion
for minimalism

FROM THE FAR NORTH TO THE CAPITAL: Designer Monica Förster, who grew up in Dorotea, a small town in Lapland, established her own design studio in Stockholm in 1999. Her portfolio is vast: cutlery for Gense, crockery for Rörstrand, chairs for Zanat, timber bowls for the Icehotel, coffee tables for Swedese and even an inflatable room for Offect. Monica Förster's curiosity and passion for form and function have taken her all the way to Sweden's design elite, and her designs are already regarded as future classics. She regularly collects awards for innovative products and was named Designer of the Year by the Swedish interior design magazine Elle Decoration in 2015. We interviewed her to find out how she converts an idea into a successful product.

Tell us a little about your work as a designer. What exactly is it that you do?

In my work, I design furniture and products on order together with my team. I don't often develop products on my own initiative. As a creative director, I also help large companies to develop, change or update their brand and language of form. This supports the client in moving their company forward in a strategical, creative direction.

What makes your work so exciting?

We work with many different clients, and each project has interesting aspects. I'm naturally a very curious person who enjoys most things. That's why Monica Förster Design Studio will essentially work on anything, from jewellery through to the operator's seat in an innovative Volvo excavator.

Can you describe one of your recent projects?

In 2018, we worked on three Christmas collections for the Danish jewellery and design label Georg Jensen. These collections – Matrix, Tunes and Christmas Collectibles – comprise vases, bowls and various candleholders.

How does your studio approach a new project?

We always start by researching very thoroughly. I visit the company and have a close look at their production processes and archives. I do everything I need to get an accurate feeling for the company. After all, we develop products that will be manufactured in large quantities later on. At the same time, each company is unique, and that's something we want to convey in our products.

What makes your style typically 'Monica Förster'?

My studio has a very strong basis in Scandinavian expression. I call it 'humanist minimalism'. Our work starts from a concept, an idea.

I always ask why something should be done. Each project is unique because we start anew from each client. Form, colour and materials come later – these are the elements that will reinforce the idea. But while each product starts from a very different basis, all of my projects have a common denominator, which is this overarching Scandinavian way of expressing design.

What makes Scandinavian design unique? Why is it so popular?

I think that Scandinavian design is easily accessible, functional and well suited for many environments. It's restrained and doesn't hog a space. With its minimalist language of form, Scandinavian design lasts through decades while staying contemporary. However, this comes with the risk that ultimately everything might look the same.

Tell us more about your background. Where does your interest in form and function come from?

I grew up in a family where everybody worked creatively in one way or another. My father was a chef, and my mother a painter. We discussed experimental ideas over dinner – that was perfectly normal for us. I'm now in charge of this legacy, but have chosen a different medium to express myself in.

What does your home look like? What's your personal taste in interior design?

My home is a home for family and friends, where you can meet and have fun. But serenity and harmony are also very important to me.

What's your relationship to Norrmalm?

My son goes to school here. Students in his class can see St. John's Church from the classroom windows – that's a really nice touch. I also love all the Asian shops and restaurants in the area.

What are your must-see places for design fans in and around Stockholm?

I'd recommend a visit to the Skogskyrkogården woodland cemetery, which was designed by the architect Gunnar Asplund and is on the UNESCO World Heritage list. Also, we have a Svenskt Tenn store (p. 76) here in Stockholm, the only one worldwide! For vintage shopping I recommend Modernity (Sibyllegatan 6). Nearby there's also Asplund, a good furniture shop (Sibyllegatan 31). And just a street further along you'll find Nordiska Galleriet (p. 90), a must for furniture and design products by Swedish and international high-end brands.

KAFFE
BOKEN

35 Rörstrand

Sweden's oldest porcelain manufacturer
has been making fine ceramics since
1726. Dozens of prominent Swedish
designers, including architect Ferdinand
Boberg, artist Isaac Grünewald and
fashion designer Filippa K, have created
collections for the company. Monica
Förster designed the Inwhite collection,
which received the Elle Decoration
magazine's Product of the Year award
for tableware in 2015. The typically
minimalist series of white cups, plates
and bowls is a true modern classic.
Kungsgatan 1
www.rorstrand.se

With fountains, a stage for events, cafés and plenty of greenery, Kungsträdgården city park could be described as Stockholm's playground.

Lots of bars and night clubs are located around Stureplan square.

WHERE THE RICH
AND BEAUTIFUL GO:
ÖSTERMALM

Stockholm's most upmarket suburb is characterised by late 19th-century town palaces, green boulevards and laneways with chic bars, boutiques and restaurants. It is also home to the National Theatre and some major museums and galleries. The area around Stureplan square with its well-known concrete 'Mushroom' offers great nightlife with bars and VIP clubs. Numerous design stores, above all Svenskt Tenn, are evidence that residents value beautiful homes and interiors. Many restaurants are dedicated to Swedish cuisine, with their kitchens transforming local ingredients into creative, unique dishes, while the market hall, a treasure trove of Nordic delicacies, whets the appetite for more.

Shopping

1 Svenskt Tenn
2 Palmgrens
4 Malmstenbutiken
5 Blue Billie
6 Sturegallerian
8 Balmuir
9 H&M Karlaplan
11 Rönnells Antikvariat
12 Nordiska Galleriet
13 Oscar & Clothilde
16 Dusty Deco

Eating

3 Hillenberg
10 Panini Internazionale
14 Östermalms Saluhall
15 Broms
17 Hantverket
20 Speceriet

Nightlife

7 Mikkeller
18 Penny & Bill

Hotel

19 Ett Hem

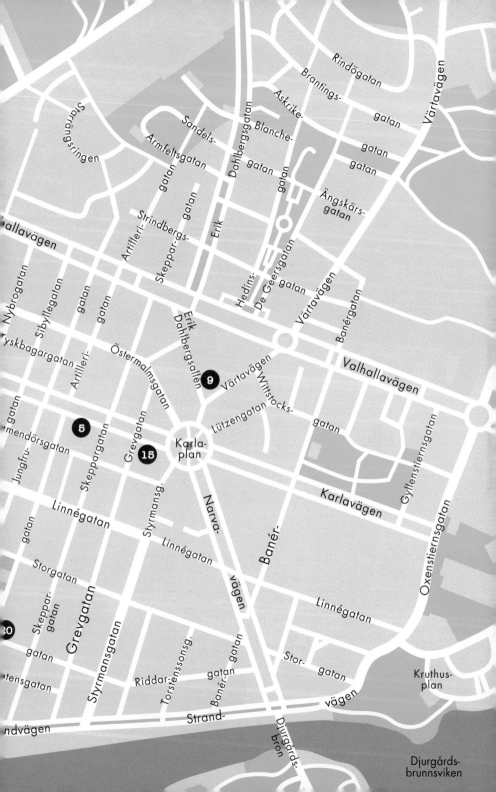

1 Svenskt Tenn

Swedish design from way back: Svenskt
Tenn has been a classic ever since the
entrepreneur Estrid Ericsson joined forces
with the Austrian architect Josef Frank
in 1934. Frank designed the company's
furniture and fabrics in the distinctive
flowery patterns still found in virtually
every Swedish home even today. This
large store in a top location stocks not
only furniture, but also a huge selection
of more portable home accessories.
Its recently opened delightful tea salon
on the first floor features furniture and
crockery by Svenskt Tenn.
Strandvägen 5
www.svenskttenn.se

2 Palmgrens

Palmgrens is a Swedish institution for anything to do with leather goods. The brand is renowned for simple, timeless handbags, from small shoulder bags for going out to stylish totes and roomy shoppers for every day. Part of each collection incorporates rattan details, a tradition that goes back to the 1950s. The company's history dates back even further to when Johannes Palmgren founded a saddlery in this very street in 1896. This background is commemorated by both the saddle in the company logo and a large wooden horse in the store.

Sibyllegatan 7
www.palmgrens.se

3 Hillenberg

In this stylish restaurant, award-winning chef Niklas Ekstedt fuses Mediterranean and Nordic influences to create a delightful fine-dining experience. Whether for a quick lunch, a relaxed dinner or just a cocktail at the bar, Hillenberg is always worth a visit. It also has a well-stocked wine cellar, and every Wednesday the restaurant's sommelier opens a few bottles of good wine for a degustation. If you want to taste some wine on your own, we recommend the affiliated wine café Tyge & Sessil just around the corner (entrance at Brahegatan 4).
Humlegårdsgatan 14
www.hillenberg.se

4 Malmstenbutiken

Carl Malmsten, one of Sweden's best-known furniture designers, opened this store on Strandvägen boulevard in 1940. His timeless designs, inspired by the elegant Swedish Grace style of the 1920s, are still much in demand 50 years after Malmsten's death. The current range includes not only original Carl Malmsten designs, but also creative innovations and Swedish design classics made of glass, porcelain, fabrics and leather. The store is a treasure trove for design fans, not least because Malmsten's grandchildren have preserved his legacy very carefully.
Strandvägen 5 B
www.malmsten.se

5 Blue Billie

Blue Billie, a jewellery label founded in 2015, is tucked away in a tiny showroom. With pendants shaped like stars, letters, fruit and animals, the designs appeal to customers' playful side. There are always two collections on display, one of silver and gold-plated pieces and a more exclusive line featuring crystals and gemstones. The pendants can be combined on necklaces and bracelets. Polaroids on the walls feature the fictitious Billie, who tells her own story through jewellery.
Karlavägen 70
www.bluebillie.com

6 Sturegallerian

This exclusive shopping mall on Stureplan square is inspired by the chic arcades of Milan and full to the brim with fashion, jewellery, accessories and beauty products in about 50 stores. Discover Swedish fashion at Stylein, Stenströms, Daisy Grace and Snoot, browse the exquisite jewellery of Caroline Svedbom or visit wellness store Idyllien for natural skincare from Gotland island. A dozen bistros and cafés serve refreshments; Brasserie Tures in the glass-ceilinged courtyard is particularly beautiful.

Stureplan 4
www.sturegallerian.se

7 Mikkeller

The Danish microbrewery Mikkeller was only founded in 2006, but Mikkel Borg Bjergsø's hipster beers are already served in 50 branded bars from Singapore to San Francisco. The brand's Stockholm watering hole opened in 2017 for all fans of a cool Sture Pils or Berliner Weisse Blood Orange. The bar serves local Swedish favourites as well as Mikkeller's own beers. With a total of 24 different beers on draught and a minimalist yet cosy interior, Mikkeller shows that upmarket Östermalm can (and sometimes wants to) be quite relaxed.
Brahegatan 3
www.mikkeller.dk

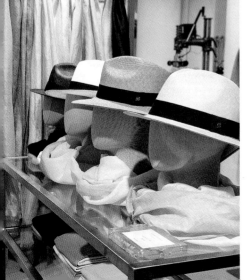

8 Balmuir

This label for exclusive fashion and home accessories hails from Finland. For women, it has highly covetable pastel-coloured bags, scarves and hats, and for men there are classic leather goods for the office and home. Some products are made of exotic, ethically produced materials such as salmon leather and alpaca skins, while bathrobes and towels give the collection a flair of Finnish sauna culture. The brand is named after the golf course where Balmuir founders Heidi and Juha Jaara met, and this is its only store outside Finland.

Grev Turegatan 8
www.balmuir.com

9 H&M Karlaplan

H&M opened its first concept store in Östermalm, where the Swedish fashion brand presents its collection in an open, airy space with plenty of room and light. Clothes are neatly displayed in delicate shelves and on stands rather than on rotating racks. Fashion, accessories and furnishings are all presented together arranged by colour, mood and occasion rather than by product type. Collaborations with artists and cafés add a special touch of exclusivity.

Karlaplan 13
www.hm.com

10 Panini Internazionale

Founded in Stockholm, this fast-food chain has in fact nothing to do with Italy, despite the name. It serves a typically Nordic selection of creatively put together salads, sandwiches and sweet pastries, and a takeaway coffee costs only seven kronas. Many locals working in the nearby offices come here for relaxed lunchtime meetings. On weekdays, the café serves a breakfast buffet until 10 am, where customers have a choice of divine sourdough sandwiches, juices and muesli.

Sibyllegatan 27
www.panini.nu

11 Rönnells Antikvariat

Opened in 1929, this antiquarian book-
shop has been a cornerstone of Stockholm's literary scene ever since. It stocks
an impressive selection of second-hand
books, including rare and out-of-print
titles, over two floors. Most of its range
is dedicated to fiction, the arts and
academic literature. Rönnells is also an
independent publisher of books and
music and hosts readings, signings and
even concerts every month except July.
The store has been struggling for years –
by shopping here, you're supporting an
important piece of reading culture.
Birger Jarlsgatan 32 B
www.ronnells.se

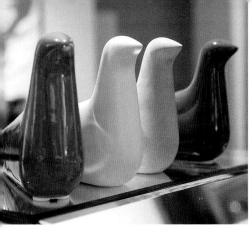

12 Nordiska Galleriet

This designer heaven, home to a remarkable selection of furniture by renowned designers and manufacturers from Scandinavia, Italy, the UK and France, was established in 1912. Its range is evenly divided between classic furnishings and contemporary designs. If you're interested in the formal language of modernism and its leading representatives such as Arne Jacobsen, Bruno Mathsson and Le Corbusier, you're in the right place. The contemporary design scene is represented by Monica Förster, Ilse Crawford and the Claesson Koivisto Rune trio.
Nybrogatan 11
www.nordiskagalleriet.se

13 Oscar & Clothilde

This store is conceptualised around the idea of two fictitious travellers bringing back exquisite furniture and home decorations from faraway lands. Apparently Oscar and Clothilde are also time travellers, as the store also stocks pieces styled after the Rococo to the colonial period. But this is all about beauty, not about geographical or historical accuracy. The store is a colourful collection of delightful, original and unusual pieces – and therefore quite the opposite of Scandinavian minimalism.

Birger Jarlsgatan 27
www.oscarclothilde.com

14 Östermalms Saluhall

Stockholm's culinary heart has been beating at this market hall on Östermalmstorg square since 1888. Here, a dozen family businesses treat gourmets to Swedish delicacies, including cheeses, reindeer and elk sausages, fish and seafood. Around the market stalls there is also a great choice of cafés and restaurants if you'd like to indulge right there and then. Among them is Lisa Elmqvist, the seafood purveyor to the Royal Court. Seafood fans will find her fish soup, and dishes featuring sole, salmon and herring, entirely unforgettable.

Östermalmstorg

www.ostermalmshallen.se

15 Broms

One of Stockholm's best breakfast cafés is right on the green Karlaplan square. Order either the set breakfast or put together your own perfect start to the day from the café's creative, fruit-inspired dishes. Choose from chia pudding with goji berries and açai bowls with muesli and coconut, as well as delicious sandwiches. On weekends, Broms serves brunch à la carte, and on weekdays this is a good place for an inexpensive lunch. If you drop by in the evening, you'll find an international menu on offer.

Karlavägen 76
www.bromskarlaplan.se

16 Dusty Deco

This home furnishing store, which stocks unique furniture, carpets and works of art as well as some more portable accessories, is located in a former industrial building. The selection is hand-picked by the store owners, whom you'll often find handling boxes of new treasures, always happy to chat about design. This urban yet relaxed store features different areas where pieces are displayed together as creative suggestions for how to combine them. With its eclectic mix of classics and modern works, the space has the feel of a design gallery.
Brahegatan 21
https://dustydeco.com

17 Hantverket

Hantverket is an insider tip for fans of modern Nordic cuisine. Instead of ordering a conventional entrée and a main, you're invited to order four or five smaller à la carte dishes. Innovative combinations of flavours extend foodies' culinary horizons and are evidence of a true passion for cooking as a craft (*handverket*). Guests are seated in a carefully and cosily designed space with plenty of wood, works of art and planted walls. A glass front lets you look out over a green courtyard.

Sturegatan 15
www.restauranghantverket.se

18 Penny & Bill

This stylish, contemporary cocktail bar right among Östermalm's exclusive stores is a perfect place for post-shopping recovery in the quiet indoor space or at one of the outdoor tables. Cocktails are categorised as either 'sour & fresh' or 'strong & intense' to make the selection easier. Penny & Bill is one of gourmet chef Henrik Norström's brainchilds, so it's also well worth checking out the menu – this gastrobar serves not only excellent drinks, but also perfectly matched bar food prepared from local ingredients.

Grev Turegatan 30
www.pennyandbill.se

19 Ett Hem

You'll find Stockholm's most exclusive boutique hotel a little off the city centre, in among charming late 19th-century townhouses in the quiet residential suburb of Lärkstaden. The British designer Ilse Crawford has converted one of these residences into a hotel where you'll feel at home immediately. Guests are treated to an inviting library and a lounge room with corner bar, and breakfast is served in the orangerie – definitely no soulless reception area here. The hotel's twelve rooms feature simple designs, but each and every detail is of outstanding quality.
Sköldungagatan 2
www.etthem.se

JACOB HOLMSTRÖM & ANTON BJUHR

Two restaurateurs with a passion for new Swedish cuisine

THE CHEFS JACOB HOLMSTRÖM AND ANTON BJUHR run two successful restaurants in Östermalm. Gastrologik was awarded a Michelin star in 2013 and is renowned among gourmets all over the world for its creative dishes prepared with Swedish ingredients. Right next door, its more casual sibling Speceriet invites diners to enjoy a more relaxed atmosphere. Jacob Holmström tells us the story behind Stockholm's most successful culinary duo, their philosophy and how the two restaurants complement each other.

You operate two very different restaurants right next to each other in Östermalm. How did this happen?

We first opened our gourmet restaurant Gastrologik back in 2011. The restaurant next door was part of it right from the start, but we initially used it for a shop with a small café corner. Our idea was to sell the ingredients that we also used to create our restaurant dishes. Hence the name, as Speceriet simply means 'grocery store'. But we soon realised that what people were after were cooked dishes rather than ingredients, and that's why we converted the shop into a lunch restaurant. It complements Gastrologik perfectly, because people go to gourmet restaurants for dinner and not for lunch. When Jonas, who was our chef at Gastrologik for a long time, took over the Speceriet kitchen, we started to serve dinner there as well.

Aren't you competing with yourself as a result?

Quite the opposite. Gastrologik is a restaurant for special occasions. People might go there once a year, or perhaps only once a lifetime. Many of our guests there are international gourmet travellers and not locals. Speceriet, in contrast, is somewhere you can go to any day. For lunch, we mainly have people working in Östermalm, and then for dinner we get local residents. Or those who couldn't get a table at Gastrologik.

Are you booked out a long time ahead?

Gastrologik is booked out a month in advance. Many tourists don't plan that far ahead, and then Speceriet is a great alternative for a spontaneous visit. But Speceriet is quite small, so it's always better to call a day ahead to make a booking.

What do the two places have in common?

Actually everything, except the presentation. Both restaurants share the same philosophy. We use the same ingredients and order from the same suppliers. At Speceriet, diners eat à la carte, while at Gastrologik all guests are served our 20-course degustation menu. Being a gourmet restaurant, Gastrologik uses genuine specialty ingredients, but as a result some rarities also cross over to the Speceriet kitchen. This is why Spenceriet is incredible value for money. Guests get to enjoy dishes that other restaurants in the middle price range simply can't prepare.

Obviously you're following the Stockholm restaurant scene. Which trends do you see?

I love the broad range. You can eat very well in many restaurants, not only those that do fine dining. Following on from the trendy New Nordic cuisine, which I believe was a bit overdone, there are now plenty of exciting international restaurants, including Mexican ones, for example.

Would you still describe your restaurants as serving New Nordic cuisine?

We'd rather call it New Swedish cuisine. We only use Swedish ingredients; that's something we're very particular about.

Do you have a signature dish?

At Gastrologik, the menu always has a dish that features Norway lobster. In spring, we serve it with fresh herbs and a crème made out of the lobster head, and in winter we combine it with fennel. There is no one signature dish, because we cook with seasonal ingredients.

The Sami, Sweden's indigenous people, follow eight instead of four seasons. Do you do that too?

It's true that Sweden has a number of relatively short periods with different climatic conditions. In our kitchen we could identify even more than eight if we wanted to. But we think in terms of ingredients instead of seasons, with each vegetable having its own season. You could say that we have hundreds of seasons, depending on what's ripe when and what sort of combinations this allows.

What do you think of Östermalm?

It's perfect for our restaurants because it's very accessible yet we're in a quiet street. Östermalm is generally a quiet suburb, except for the party scene around Stureplan square. I like the grand old buildings. Plus we have amazing nature around the corner, as Djurgården island is close by.

Can you share a few tips for a great visit to Stockholm?

I love walking along Söder Mälarstrand boulevard. If you take any of the paths further up the hill near Slussen, you get fabulous views of the water and Kungsholmen. I enjoy eating at Babette's (Roslagsgatan 6), where you can sit outside in summer.

20 Speceriet

The casual sibling of celebrated Michelin-starred restaurant Gastrologik gives guests a taste of Swedish fine dining without costing them their entire holiday budget or hours and hours of time. Try the wonderful, melt-in-the-mouth lamb or pickled salmon, made from a recipe by head chef Jacob Holmström's grandfather. This intimate restaurant, whose Nordic design matches its cuisine, seats only about 20 people, and booking ahead is a must. On weekdays, Speceriet serves an inexpensive lunch menu.
Artillerigatan 14
www.speceriet.se

You'll find a number of restaurant and bar boats anchored along Strandvägen boulevard.

No trip to Sweden would be complete without meatballs.

RELAXED AND HIP:
SOFO

Since the 2000s, the laneways 'south of Folkungagatan' have evolved into a dynamic scene of small, owner-run boutiques, shops, pubs and bars. Ambitious young entrepreneurs keep developing new ideas that combine stores with cafés, bistros with supermarkets and design objects with wines. The old timber houses and crooked lanes around Nytorget square remind us that this was once a humble working-class area. Later on, students moved in, and these days SoFo has transformed entirely from alternative quarter to hipster hangout. Bloggers and fashion magazine editors regularly scout the area for the latest promising labels and trends.

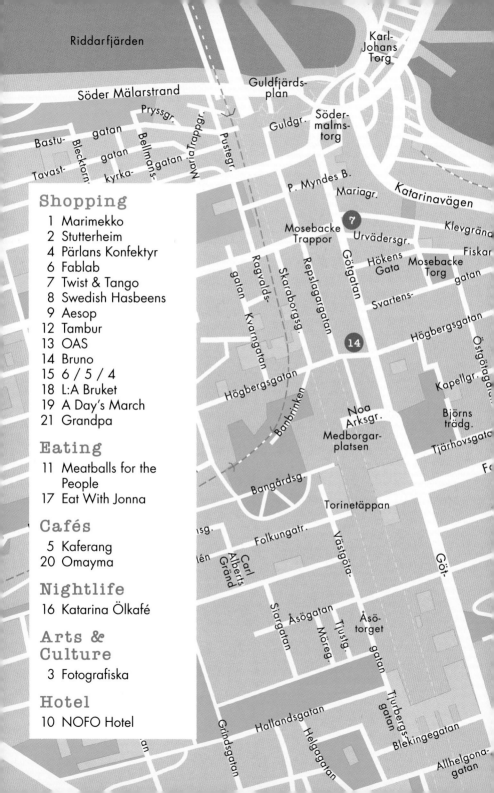

Shopping

1 Marimekko
2 Stutterheim
4 Pärlans Konfektyr
6 Fablab
7 Twist & Tango
8 Swedish Hasbeens
9 Aesop
12 Tambur
13 OAS
14 Bruno
15 6 / 5 / 4
18 L:A Bruket
19 A Day's March
21 Grandpa

Eating

11 Meatballs for the People
17 Eat With Jonna

Cafés

5 Kaferang
20 Omayma

Nightlife

16 Katarina Ölkafé

Arts & Culture

3 Fotografiska

Hotel

10 NOFO Hotel

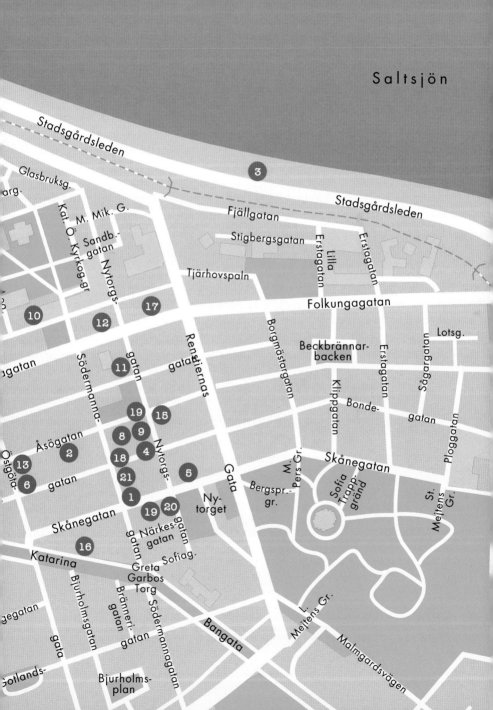

Strömmen

Saltsjön

Stadsgårdsleden

Glasbruksg.

arg.

Kat. Ö. Kyrkog.-gr

M. Mik. G.

Sandb.-gatan

Nytorgs-

Stadsgårdsleden

③

Fjällgatan

Stigbergsgatan

Erstagatan

Lilla

Erstagatan

Tjärhovspaln

Folkungagatan

⑩

⑫

⑰

gatan

Södermanna-

agatan

⑪

Renstiernas

gatan

Borgmästaregatan

Beckbrännar-
backen

Erstagatan

Lotsg.

Sågargatan

Åsögatan

⑲ ⑮

⑧ ⑨

② ⑬

Nytorgs-

④

⑱

Ö. Götgö-

⑥

gatan

⑤

㉑

①

Gata

Nytorget

Bergspr.-
gr.

M. Pers Gr.

Klippgatan

Bonde-

gatan

Skånegatan

Sofia
Trapp-
gränd

Ploggatan

St.
Mejtens
Gr.

Skånegatan

⑲ ⑳

Närkes-
gatan

gatan

Sofiag.

Mejtens Gr.

⑯

Katarina

Greta
Garbos
Torg

Bränneri-
gatan

Södermannagatan

egatan

Bjurholmsgatan

gatan

Bangata

L.
Mejtens Gr.

Malmgårdsvägen

otlands-

gata

Bjurholms-
plan

1 Marimekko

This Finnish designer brand, founded in Helsinki in 1951, is well known for its graphic prints, which use colour sparsely but apply contrasts and striking shapes to great effect. The label's signature poppy flowers, stripes and dots stand out particularly well on dresses, bags and cushions. By the way, the brand name means 'Marie's dress'. The store sells not only its own cheerful, high-quality designs, but also glass objects and home accessories by other Finnish designers.
Skånegatan 71
www.marimekko.com

2 Stutterheim

It's not uncommon for Sweden – the south more so than the Stockholm area – to be drenched by heavy rains for weeks on end. This calls for functional yet stylish clothing, and that's where Stutterheim's rain jackets in all colours of the rainbow come in. Are you someone who underlines their irrepressible cheerfulness with pastel or vibrant colours? Or do you prefer more melancholic tones of grey and black? If so, Stutterheim coats might be an even better fit for you – the company's slogan is 'Swedish melancholy at its driest'.
Åsögatan 136
www.stutterheim.com

SWEDISH
MELANCHOLY
AT ITS DRIEST

STUTTERHEIM RAINCOATS

3 Fotografiska

If time allows you to visit only one cultural attraction, we recommend Stockholm's contemporary photography gallery. Housed in a converted customs office on the water, it showcases works by renowned Nordic and international photographers such as Martin Schoeller, David LaChapelle and Annie Leibovitz in its temporary exhibitions. Thanks to very generous opening hours (Sun–Wed 9 am–11 pm, Thu–Sat even until 1 am), you can drop by after dinner. The gallery includes a bistro with an amazing view through vast windows.

Stadsgårdshamnen 22
www.fotografiska.com

4 Pärlans Konfektyr

SoFo's sweetest address is the place to go for those with a sweet tooth and/or a penchant for retro style. The store's interior is a perfectly preserved example of 1930s Sweden, when the country worked to improve everybody's standard of living, while the rest of Europe was at war. You'll be served by women with soft blow-dried curls, wearing polka dot dresses, and there'll be jazz music in the background. Watch the confectioners through a window as they transform natural ingredients into sweet delights. Pärlans Konfektyr also sells chocolate and jams.

Nytorgsgatan 38
www.parlanskonfektyr.se

5 Kaferang

This stylish place is as skilful and credible a combination of café, restaurant and wine bar as you'll ever find. Its amazing design will captivate you immediately. Sleek lamps, wooden stools, concrete surfaces and a lot of grey create an environment of immaculate industrial chic that makes it hard to decide whether to sit inside or at one of the outdoor tables with a view of Nytorget square. With about 20 tables, Kaferang is one of SoFo's larger cafés, but plenty of staff ensure that customers are served quickly even at the busiest of times.

Skånegatan 81
www.kaferang.se

6 Fablab

For stylist and Vogue photographer Johan Svenson, his small store, a treasure chest of contemporary curios, is a playground of good design with a sense of humour. If you know your friends (very) well, you'll find unusual gifts among an eclectic selection of pithy self-help books, hipster cosmetics and little ceramic monkeys. And if you're shopping for yourself, you'll come across home accessories that you never knew existed. An online shop provides consolation for those who can't make the limited opening hours (Thursday to Sunday only).

Bondegatan 7
www.fab-lab.nu

7 Twist & Tango

This established Swedish brand offers cohesive collections of everyday women's fashion. With uni-colour classics, flattering cuts and carefully measured statement pieces, Twist & Tango's creations have definite must-have potential, because they're comfortable, sit well and can be worn at work and home. The label still retains some of the casual, relaxed vibe of Gothenburg, the port city where it was founded. Its oldest store in Stockholm surprises with an elegant interior that really allows the collection to shine.

Götgatan 9
www.twisttango.com

8 Swedish Hasbeens

These clogs have achieved cult status in Sweden, and are even worn by Hollywood stars. One of their most famous fans is Sarah Jessica Parker, who reportedly owns several pairs. The wooden soles, which are available in different heel heights, are amazingly comfortable, and the leather comes in different colours and textures, from sleek to braided.
Visit the flagship store on Södermalm for the current collection, or the outlet store in the old town (Västerlånggatan 65, see map p. 180, D) for past collections at half price, including in popular sizes.
Flagship store: Nytorgsgatan 36 A
www.swedishhasbeens.com

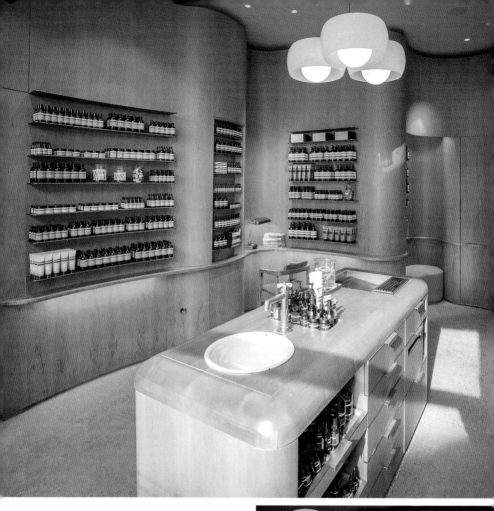

9 Aesop

Once upon a time there was… skincare. If fairy tales had pharmacies, they'd probably look like this branch of the Australian skincare company Aesop: curved walls, a pleasantly fresh scent and lighting that brings a soft glow to the wooden surfaces. Behind the counter you'll find a contemporary version of the fairy godmother handling plant concoctions and providing urban princesses with beautifully packaged potions for their stressed skins. These work their magic after a few applications – and their effect won't vanish at the stroke of midnight.

Nytorgsgatan 36
www.aesop.com

10 NOFO Hotel

With each of its 48 rooms being furnished differently, this hotel exemplifies the open, creative spirit of modern SoFo. You might find yourself on a retro couch in front of floral wallpaper, or in a velvet-laden boudoir with lace curtains. Despite their diversity, all rooms offer the same high standard, and the hotel is a favourite among musicians playing gigs at one of the nearby venues. The green courtyard makes you forget that you're in the heart of Stockholm's hippest suburb. Visit the wine bar for a selection of organic wines.
Tjärhovsgatan 11
www.nofohotel.se

11 Meatballs for the People

Could there be anything more typically Swedish than meatballs with potatoes and lingonberries? This eatery always has the classic version on the menu, but there is also an ever-changing selection of creative variations with unusual sides and sauces, plus fish balls and vegetarian alternatives. This is definitely not a touristy place; instead, you'll sit next to locals in this rustic yet cool restaurant. Come here for inexpensive weekday lunches for about 140 krona (from 11 am to 5 pm).

Nytorgsgatan 30
www.meatball.se

Ways to my heart:

1. Buy me meatballs

2. Make me meatballs

3. BE a meatball

WE LOVE MEATBALL

12 Tambur

Tambur is no bigger than a small apartment and feels more like somebody's home than a store, especially as its rooms are furnished by themes. Yet it stocks an astounding range of Swedish design items for all aspects of home living, from kitchen appliances to organic cotton bed linen, watering cans and glass jugs. One of Tambur's fundamental principles is sustainability, and the entire range is locally made and free from chemicals. The store is only open from Wednesday to Saturday.

Folkungagatan 85
www.tamburstore.se

13 OAS

Swimwear in classic cuts and playful patterns: OAS founder Oliver Adam Sebastian's recipe for success is strikingly simple. Having delighted holidaymakers in 15 countries from Italy to Asia with his designs for years, he opened his first store in Sweden in 2018. With roughly rendered walls and Mediterranean decorations, it evokes the feeling of a Spanish hacienda. Stockholm does have hot summer days, and there are swimming spots right in the city. Who knows, you might even get your pineapple bikini or cactus print boardshorts wet in Lake Mälaren!
Åsögatan 128
www.oascompany.com

14 Bruno

A visit to Bruno's can save you valuable shopping time, as this stylish arcade is home to Swedish labels HOPE, Whyred, Filippa K and J. Lindeberg as well as the multi-brand store Aplace, which sells a wide range of Scandinavian fashion.
If you need sustenance at any time during or after your shopping spree, there's Ljunggren, an airy bistro where fashion-forward locals meet after work. On weekends the bistro turns into a nightclub, and on Sundays it serves an Asian-inspired lunch menu.
Götgatan 36
www.brunogotgatsbacken.se

15 6 / 5 / 4

This concept store, founded in 2009, was originally all about surfing, but gradually expanded its range to include a number of unusual outdoor products. Shop here for surfboards, swimwear and relaxed fashion as well as tents, thermos flasks and useful gadgets for outdoor cooking. The store also includes a bar and organic coffee shop. Some days you might be welcomed by a sausage sizzle or an impromptu concert in front of the store – it's a very chilled meeting point that really embodies the SoFo character.

Nytorgsgatan 27
www.654.se

16 Katarina Ölkafé

Stockholm craft beer meets Jewish cuisine from New York. The result: a haven for body and soul. This small 'beer café' (*öl* is Swedish for 'beer') does not pour established hipster beers, but works with microbreweries, some of them so small that labels are copied and attached by the enthusiastic brewers themselves. The American beer sommelier is happy to help you choose. Food includes generous pastrami sandwiches with sauerkraut and mustard (feel free to share – one feeds two people) or a typically American mac and cheese.

Katarina Bangata 27
www.katarinaolkafe.se

The northernmost section of Götgatan is a popular pedestrian and cycling mall.

17 Eat With Jonna

Jonna's cheerful nature and lovingly prepared sandwiches have made this place a SoFo institution. Her generous and unusual *smörrebröd* creations with salmon, roast beef or homemade liver paté are quite unforgettable, and the café's cool kitsch interior is just as memorable: Jonna's enthusiasm for pink, yellow and orange seems to know no bounds, with a fake fur armchair here and a shelf stacked with books and funny figurines there. With its personable service and cheeky interior, this café (open Wednesday to Sunday) is one of a kind.
Folkungatan 95
www.eatwithjonna.se

18 L:A Bruket

The products by L:A Bruket prove that innovative skincare can be chemical-free. The brand, founded in 2008 in the Swedish spa town of Varberg on the country's west coast, uses seaweed from the North Sea, among other ingredients. Its founders Monica Kylén and Mats Johansson started with a face cream to protect the skin of fishermen, sailors and others working outdoors against the harsh air and winds. They've since expanded their range significantly so that their flagship store is now full of beautiful flasks, tubes and tins, also for city slickers.

Södermannagatan 21
www.labruket.se

19 A Day's March

This Stockholm brand is synonymous with high-quality menswear basics. Its minimalist pieces are only available online or in its branded stores, of which there are a total of five in Sweden and London. As the label's founders sell their designs directly, they are able to offer them at a somewhat lower price than stores that stock different brands and need to pay commissions. The name references the idea of a day's march in the army. The brand wants to accompany its customers throughout the day, wherever they go: to the office, on holiday or out on the town.
Nytorgsgatan 36
www.adaysmarch.com

20 Omayma

Love, patience, care – Omayma is an Arabic girl's name that encompasses all of these virtues. These same virtues are also embodied by the café, rightly renowned for its friendly staff and selection of organic dishes. Enjoy the food with fabulous coffee, healthy juices or more unusual drinks such as a beetroot or charcoal latte. Omayma is popular among Södermalm locals for its all-day breakfast: choose between different sandwiches or cashew yoghurt with mango sauce and coconut crumble, for example.

Skånegatan 92
www.omayma.se

A great view: Södermalm's grand buildings rise high above the water.

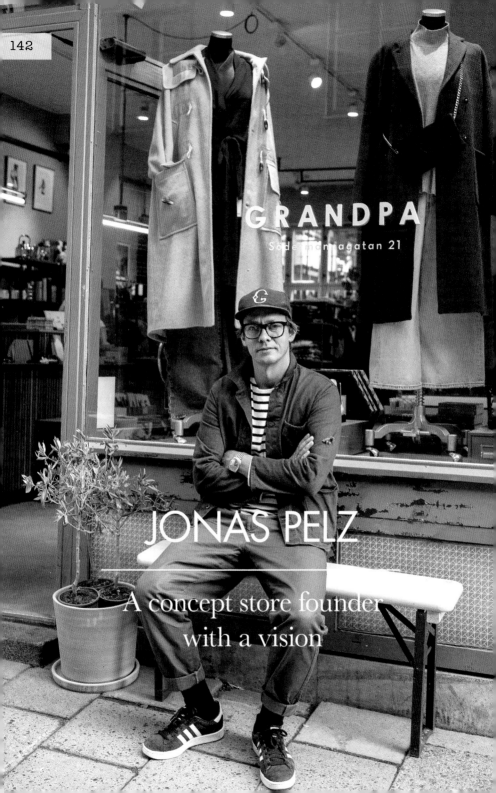

JONAS PELZ

A concept store founder
with a vision

GRANDPA IS A CONCEPT STORE par excellence. It treats design-loving customers to a hand-picked selection of fashion, home accessories, stationery, books and art works from across Scandinavia in a sophisticated ambience, with knowledgeable staff happy to provide personalised advice. This successful shopping experience is the brainchild of three Stockholmers who appreciate good service. Co-founder Jonas Pelz tells the story of Grandpa and SoFo and shares his favourite places in this hip suburb.

The first Grandpa opened in SoFo in 2003. Was this a cool area even then?

Not at all. There were only few shops, most of them very traditional. There were some artisans and a weaving company, for example, but the name 'SoFo' already existed.

What did it mean at the time?

It was a reference to SoHo in New York, the trendy suburb 'south of Houston Street'. And SoFo stands for 'south of Folkungagatan'. But that was quite ironic at the time – SoFo was nowhere near as cool as New York. That only started with the SoFo nights on the last Thursday of each month. The Grandpa team was one of the driving forces behind this concept, and we tried to attract more shops to SoFo. The more selection people have, the better. The fact that the area had a name even then helped local shop owners and restaurateurs to get together and get things happening.

What inspired you to found Grandpa?

There were three founders: Anders, Martin and I. We all have a background in service, love Stockholm and wanted – that was our very vague idea – to create a place that people would really love to go to. The obvious choices were to start a new café, restaurant or hotel. None of us had ever worked with fashion or furnishings, not even selling it. But we were interested in this field, and so we combined our experience in service to develop a new shopping concept.

Where does the name come from?

Our co-founder Anders once worked in a restaurant, many years ago, and his colleagues nicknamed him 'grandpa'. I have no idea why. But we all agreed that this would be the name for our project.

What's the concept that underpins Grandpa?

You can do so much more than shop: there are exhibitions, concerts and events. Also, the fact that Södermannagatan street is now a pedestrian mall goes back to one of our initiatives. We negotiated with the city council for a long time to make the shopping experience more pleasant. Service, atmosphere and inspiration are Grandpa's fundamental values. Today, the concept is very mature and professional. But it still reflects our fundamental values, and we want everybody to feel welcome.

Who shops at Grandpa's?

While our philosophy is that Grandpa's is just as much a place for Östermalm fashionistas in their 20s as it is for plumbers from the suburbs in their 50s, we do have a clear target group, which is city people around the age of 30. Our customers shop consciously, think critically and are involved in environmental and social issues. Many of our customers don't want to browse our store anonymously; they rather seek to engage with our staff.

You have two stores in Stockholm and one each in Gothenburg and Malmö. Are you planning to open more?

Not in Sweden, but maybe abroad. I'd be intrigued to go to Germany, because we have many customers from there, both in-store and online. Berlin would be an obvious choice, sure, but I think that Grandpa could fill a substantial niche in Hamburg as well. I'm also following the scene in London. I'm totally passionate about the concept of sharing the Scandinavian way of life and Scandinavian fashion.

What makes SoFo unique?

This suburb keeps evolving and renewing itself. There are no large chains, only small stores, and SoFo just feels authentic. Plus it has the atmosphere of a small town. This is also enhanced by the townscape: there are many old buildings, only a few high-rise ones, and the streets are narrow and quiet. I lived in SoFo for ten years and still feel totally at home here.

What are your favourite stores in SoFo?

Tambur (p. 128) has beautiful, sophisticated furnishings, and 6 / 5 / 4 (p. 132) stocks an amazing mixture of surfing gear and fashion. I also recommend a visit to Konstig (Åsögatan 124), a bookstore that also sells posters. The Älskade Traditioner café (Södermannagatan 42) is very cute. It's all fitted out in the style of the 1950s and serves utterly delicious milkshakes. It's quirky, friendly and just different.

What do you suggest people should do on a visit to Stockholm?

I recommend hiring a bike and cycling from Södermalm to Skeppsholmen island, where you can visit the Moderna Museet (see p. 198) and enjoy a good lunch. After lunch, keep cycling to Djurgården island or along Norr Mälarstrand boulevard. Having water and nature everywhere is what makes Stockholm unique.

21 Grandpa

This hip concept store has sold Scandinavian fashion, accessories and design objects since 2003. It stocks a huge selection of brands ranging from established labels such as Rodebjer, HAY, Sandqvist and Han Kjøbenhavn to smaller designers like Iris Hantverk and Kavat. There are also innovative IT products, books, posters and desktop accessories. Come here for an excellent, appealingly presented overview of Scandinavian lifestyle products, and you can even take your favourite item(s) home!

Södermannagatan 21

www.grandpastore.com

*Djurgården island is where
Stockholm breathes nature.
You won't find shops here, only
museums and walking paths.*

Shopping

1 Uniforms for the Dedicated
2 L'Homme Rouge
4 Our Legacy
5 Filippa K Second Hand
7 Papercut
8 Sandqvist
10 Nitty Gritty
15 Lakritsroten
17 Herr Judit
20 Brandstationen
C Mini Rodini Treasures (outlet; flagship store see p. 212)

Eating

14 Kalf & Hansen

Cafés

3 Drop Coffee Roasters
6 Café Rival

Nightlife

9 Hommage
11 Folkbaren
13 Tjoget
16 Morfar Ginko
18 Hornhuset

Arts & Culture

12 'Puckeln' gallery haven
19 Hornstulls Marknad

THE FASHIONABLE WEST OF SÖDERMALM:
MARIATORGET & HORNST

The busy squares of Mariatorget and Hornstull form the two poles of Hornsgatan street. Visit this part of Stockholm at the western end of Södermalm island for independent stores and award-winning cocktail bars similar to what you find in hip SoFo. The range is just as diverse too, even though this suburb doesn't (yet) have a cool name. Krukmakargatan street, where some emerging labels started off, is fashion central, with one boutique next to another, and at the eastern end of Hornsgatan street you'll find about a dozen art galleries. On weekends, locals gather along the Hornstulls Strand promenade to browse through vintage fashion and sample delicious bites from food trucks.

1 Uniforms for the Dedicated

This menswear label, which makes high-quality, timeless pieces out of organic cotton and recycled fabrics, was founded in 2008. Designer Rasmus Wingårdh fuses elements of sports, military and functional wear, and adds a touch of elegance and pared-back cuts to make trendy streetwear. His one- or two-coloured shirts, sweaters and trousers create a perfect, relaxed uniform to be worn day in and out. The collection is small and sophisticated, with outfits for every day and special occasions.
Krukmakargatan 24
www.uniformsforthededicated.com

2 L'Homme Rouge

This fashion label for contemporary menswear started in 2013 as an experiment by four students from Lund, who shared an interest in design, art and culture. The collection of 'The Red Man' has grown from a modest selection of beanies to a full range of shirts, pants and jackets and become a powerhouse of Nordic fashion design along the way. Each collection tells a story, sometimes of dock workers, sometimes of hippies. In 2017, L'Homme Rouge was named 'Brand of the Year' by the upmarket department store NK.
Krukmakargatan 29
www.lhommerouge.com

3 Drop Coffee Roasters

After Joanna Alm and Stephen Leighton opened their café in 2009, they became curious about roasting their own coffee beans and started to dabble in their back room. Their experiment is now an internationally successful coffee roasting house that regularly collects awards at the Swedish Roasters Championship and worldwide. This is their only café so far, where fans can taste different varieties to find their personal favourite from among the range of fruity to chocolatey notes. Drop sells only organic, fairtrade coffee as a matter of course.

Wollmar Yxkullsgatan 10
www.dropcoffee.se

4 Our Legacy

This Stockholm fashion label, established in 2005, has become internationally successful with its natural, earthy colour palette, relaxed style and statement jackets. Its creations are worn by stars including John Legend and Kanye West. The brand started in this small shop on Södermalm, designed by architect Arrhov Frick with concrete surfaces and clear lines for a cool, minimalist look. Our Legacy has also been popular with women for some time, and in 2019 they finally got their own, somewhat more feminine collection.

Krukmakargatan 24
www.ourlegacy.se

5 Filippa K Second Hand

If it didn't say so on the sign, you'd probably not even notice that the fashion in this stylishly decorated store is pre-loved. Selling clothes by the popular Swedish label Filippa K, it stocks a good range of dresses, women's and men's shirts, all hand-picked and in excellent condition. Some items may even be available in several sizes. With timeless, spotless finds at inexpensive prices, plus advice from delightful staff, you only have yourself to blame if you don't visit.

Hornsgatan 77
www.filippaksecondhand.se

The tiered houses on the northern side of Södermalm show just how steep this island is.

6 Café Rival

This coffee house has plenty of room over two levels. Downstairs is the salon with a bar and dark timber furniture, accentuated by strong colours and portraits of cultural icons on the walls. If you prefer a quieter environment, take the stairs to the first floor, where pastel-coloured sofas may lead you to believe you've accidentally stepped into somebody's lounge room. The café is part of the legendary boutique hotel Rival, owned by former ABBA singer Benny Andersson and regularly visited by Swedish celebrities.
Mariatorget 1 D
www.rival.se

7 Papercut

Are you crazy about indie magazines and lifestyle books? Then this is the place for you. Papercut stocks international books and magazines, from publications by Monocle and Kinfolk to cookbooks and biographies of major contemporary personalities. The hand-picked, mostly English-language range is aimed at aficionados of fashion, design, art, travel, music and film and all those who still like the feel of turning actual pages instead of swiping screens. If that's you, you might want to check your luggage allowance before dropping by.
Krukmakargatan 24
www.papercutshop.se

8 Sandqvist

Have you ever noticed the backpacks carried by virtually every Swedophile? They're from right here. Sandqvist packs are inspired by both the pristine Nordic landscapes and urban life, meaning that they're perfectly at home in the city and in nature and will happily carry your outdoor knife and your day's shopping. The range also includes beautifully simple handbags, toiletry and travel bags. In typically Swedish fashion, the label uses organic cotton and recycled polyester as sustainable materials.

Swedenborgsgatan 3
www.sandqvist.net

9 Hommage

Stockholmers tend to drink beer, wine and bubbly a lot more than cocktails, so fans of the latter often struggle to find a good bar. Enter Hommage, a watering hole for everybody who loves to try out new flavour combinations in liquid form. The imaginative cocktails are named after famous destinations from all over the world, and the drinks menu comes on postcards. Hommage, which also includes a charming deli-bistro, is located in a former fire station, whose large, rounded windows evoke a nostalgic air.
Krukmakargatan 22
www.bar-hommage.com

10 Nitty Gritty

This fashion haven stocks an eclectic collection of Nordic and international labels, and its mix of established and newcomer brands is well worth a visit. Nitty Gritty was founded in 1991 as a courageous form of rebellion against the dominance of large department stores, which ruled the Swedish fashion scene in the early 1990s. It has been successful since, not least due to its unusual, yet consistently stylish selection. Its two separate stores for women's and men's fashion are right next to each other.
Krukmakargatan 24
www.nittygrittystore.com

11 Folkbaren

The bar next to the Stockholm Folkoperan theatre is a popular meeting point for Södermalm locals. It skilfully combines a bar and restaurant and offers space for plenty of customers over two levels. The sophisticated restaurant section alone seats 70 people. If you're only after drinks, order a delicious cocktail from the small ground-floor bar or kick back with a glass of bubbly on one of the sofas in the comfy lounge. The bar regularly hosts DJs, and its atmosphere is relaxed and friendly. In summer, the tables on the footpath are very much in demand.
Hornsgatan 72
www.folkbaren.se

12 'Puckeln' gallery haven

Puckeln means 'bump', and Stockholm's arts scene is gathered around the little hill on Hornsgatan street. There are about a dozen galleries right next to each other on the elevated section of the street opposite the yellow St. Mary-Magdalene Church. The galleries are in heritage buildings with atmospheric exhibition spaces, the oldest of which date back to the 18th century. Visit the Blås & Knåda artists' collective (established in 1975), whose 40 members create unique pieces from ceramics, glass and metal, or admire the paintings at Konst & Folk.
Hornsgatan 26

13 Tjoget

Tjoget extends across three spaces: the Mediterranean-inspired restaurant Linje Tio, the wine bar Hornstulls Bodega and the barber Roy & Son, where men can get an expert shave or a sharp haircut. The highlight of this relaxed venue is its cocktails, as Tjoget's bar staff aren't scared of exploring exotic flavours. Try the signature 'Beets by Tjoget', starring Absolut vodka, beetroot, coconut, lemon, ginger and nutmeg, and you'll understand why this bar is listed as one of the world's top 50.
Hornsbruksgatan 24
www.tjoget.com

14 Kalf & Hansen

This small corner café serves organic fast food made from local ingredients. Its healthy creations will set you back between 70 and 120 krona for eating in or taking away. Nordic dishes are served with your choice of fish, meat or veggie patties, and the drinks menu includes homemade lemonade, smoothies and beer from microbreweries. Established in 2014, Kalif & Hansen has set the benchmark for fast food: its owners have published several cookbooks, and their food is also served in the on-board restaurants of the Swedish railway.

Mariatorget 2
www.kalfochhansen.se

15 Lakritsroten

If you didn't already know that licorice can be so much more than a sticky black mass that requires an acquired taste, this store will convince you. Licorice root is a healthy ingredient that can be made into sweets, juice and salty or sour nibblies. These colourful little balls with chocolate-covered raspberry, peach or orange-flavoured licorice make lovely gifts. You're invited to taste to make your decision among the many flavours easier.
Hornsgatan 45
www.lakritsroten.se

16 Morfar Ginko

This bar is typical of Södermalm in that it is an eclectic mix of a club, bistro and champagne bar, plus it has a barber ready to put the finishing touch on gents before a night out. Morfar Ginko is a great place for mingling with locals, whether over salmon and oysters or sipping a Bellini while you see where the night will take you. With chandeliers, candles and white table linen, its interior evokes the atmosphere of Bohemian Paris. Take your time: the bar is open until 1 am daily.

Swedenborgsgatan 13
www.morfarginko.se

17 Herr Judit

This stylish second-hand shop only stocks menswear, mostly by Swedish and international designer labels. The range focuses on high quality, so that the pieces can easily get another lease of life. New accessories, as well as ties and bow ties by the proprietary label, complement the second-hand offering. Herr Judit's dedicated owners travel all over the UK, Italy and the USA to find exciting designs for fashion-forward men who don't want to spend a fortune on great style.
Hornsgatan 65
www.herrjudit.se

18 Hornhuset

The colourful high-rise building above Hornstull metro station houses four very different, but all very relaxed, food and drinks venues. Cebicheria Barranco on the ground floor serves lunch and dinner inspired by Peruvian and Mexican cooking. Above, there's the rather unusual bar Laika, where patrons don't sit at tables, but instead lounge in beds or a ball-filled pool. At Enzo's you can play a round of table football while you wait for your pizza or other Italian food. The highlight is Barrio, the rooftop summer bar.

Långholmsgatan 15 B
www.hornhuset.se

19 Hornstulls Marknad

Between April and September, the promenade along the southern side of Södermalm turns into a fair with a flea-market and an excellent range of food trucks. The wide stairs on Bergsunds Strand are the best place for sunbathing and people-watching. With daring combinations of dresses and fur vests on display next to modern takes on marine styles and Scandinavian sophistication in black and white, this is better than any fashion magazine. Some of the stalls sell Swedish design at bargain prices if you fancy trying the local potpourri style.
Hornstulls Strand 4
www.hornstullsmarknad.se

CHRISTIAN QUAGLIA

A vintage expert with
style and vision

STYLE ICON CHRISTIAN QUAGLIA manages the vintage stores Herr Judit and Brandstationen on Hornsgatan street. He happily leaves Swedish minimalist furnishings to others and instead subscribes to an out-there mixture of old and new, exoticism, colour and velvet. Christian travels all over the world and puts his connections with upmarket Stockholm to good use to acquire unique pieces for his lovingly curated stores. In our interview, he shares tips on good style in your home and wardrobe – and reminisces about special finds he's come across during his career.

Where does your love of design come from?
I've always been surrounded by fashion from a very young age. My father and all of my Italian family worked with textiles. I was involved in selecting fabrics and was allowed to touch anything, even as a child. My fascination with fabrics began as I developed a feeling for linen, silk and cotton and how they're different from synthetic materials.

Is there a particular period you specialise in?
At the Brandstationen store I want customers to experience diversity, and I love to play with the contrast between different styles and materials, new and antique. But I love Art Nouveau and Italian design from the 1950s. These periods are pure magic. You'll find these styles everywhere in the store, in jewellery as well as in vintage and new furniture. When I buy new furniture, I want it to match what's there. I like furniture with a bit of weight that will become vintage in future.

You're running two vintage stores in the same street. How did that come about?
I originally studied political science and planned to work analysing the media and democracy, but then realised that that just wasn't for me. What I really wanted to do was to open a menswear store. I was already working with the second-hand store Judit next door, which sells vintage fashion for women, and this is how the odd name 'Herr Judit' came about. In 2007, I was offered a former fire station on Krukmakargatan street, where Bar Hommage is now (p. 159), for another store, and that again determined the name. That's where I fulfilled my dream of doing something with furniture. I had no connections and didn't know much about styles and periods, but I learned as I went, and that was the best education. At the time, antiques shops specialised in particular decades, but I thought in terms of colours and shapes instead and looked for what I liked. And this is how I fuse different styles to form my own. I love it.

What makes Brandstationen unique?

This is where I can display furniture the way people might put pieces together at home. Still lives made of interiors, if you want. That's what makes Brandstationen different from other design stores, where products are lined up. I'm able to show the effect and feeling furniture and accessories can have and create when they're combined. That brings the store alive.

Where do you get your fabulous pieces?

I often buy at auctions, but even more often when I travel. I travel a lot and look for things that are as un-Swedish as possible. A great deal of my collections comes from Italy, for example lamps. I buy jewellery in the USA and UK and candle holders in Germany. What I want is to find a market that is excellent for a particular category of products. Recently I started buying via Instagram. I see my role as that of a curator. It's a lot of work, but it's enormous fun.

What is your best find?

A wonderful armchair and stylish wastepaper basket from the van der Nootska town palace on St. Paulsgatan street here on Södermalm. That's where Jean Jansson lived, the owner of the jewellery brand Hallbergs Guld. He was like Stockholm's own Great Gatsby. He had not only the city's largest private library, but also gave parties for Stockholm's high society all the time. And he collected like a maniac. He bought the house in 1900, but was later forced to sell it and move out during the 1932 crisis, after the so-called Kreuger crash.

What are your tips for creating a stylish home?

Plants! They look beautiful and create a sense of comfort and security. Generally, the current trend is towards natural materials. My favourite Instagram hashtag is urbanjungle, where you see how people create highly stylish green homes with exotic, large-leaved plants. That's also why I love Art Nouveau with its floral elements.

And what about Stockholmers' sense of fashion?

I think that Stockholmers generally dress very well. If you look at the major brands such as COS (p. 20) and Filippa K (pp. 39, 154), you notice that there's a certain framework within which fashion is contained. I'm different – I love being out there. It's like in fashion: haute couture is about as crazy as it gets, and it shows what's possible. But ultimately nobody dresses like that. Instead, people buy maybe one stand-out piece and combine it with the basics they already have.

20 Brandstationen

This vintage store describes itself as a 'toy store for adults'. Its highly covetable pieces – lovingly selected by style icon Christian Quaglia – create a relaxed, cheerful atmosphere. You'll find not only second-hand sofas, lamps and Tiffany bracelets, but also brand-new products that could very well become tomorrow's classics. When the owner isn't travelling in search of inspiration, he loves to spend time in the store and is happy to chat about design and home living trends.

Hornsgatan 64
www.herrjudit.se/brandstationen

Strandvägen promenade on Östermalm is Sweden's most exclusive address.

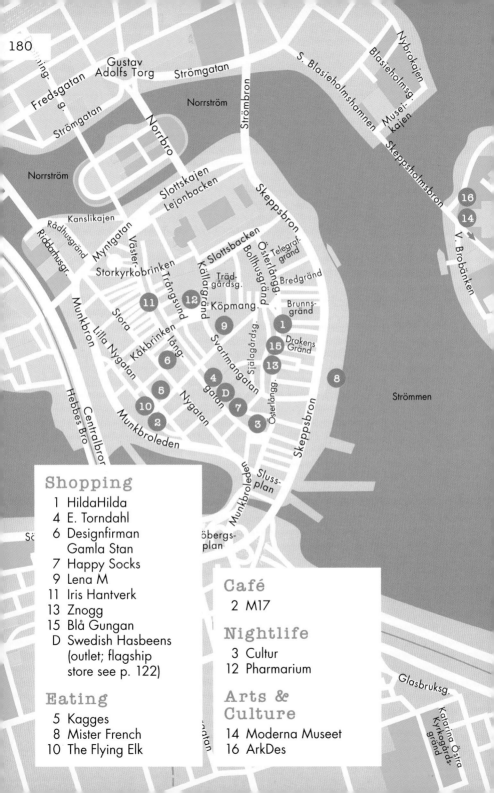

Shopping

1 HildaHilda
4 E. Torndahl
6 Designfirman
  Gamla Stan
7 Happy Socks
9 Lena M
11 Iris Hantverk
13 Znogg
15 Blå Gungan
D Swedish Hasbeens
  (outlet; flagship
  store see p. 122)

Eating

5 Kagges
8 Mister French
10 The Flying Elk

Café

2 M17

Nightlife

3 Cultur
12 Pharmarium

Arts & Culture

14 Moderna Museet
16 ArkDes

THE CITY'S CHARMING HISTORICAL HEART:
GAMLA STAN

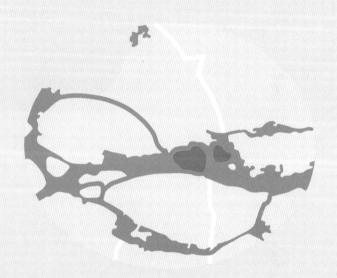

What we now call the 'old town' is where Stockholm was founded 800 years ago. The historic town centre with its red, yellow and orange buildings, narrow cobbled lanes and peaceful squares has been preserved in all of its authenticity. Visitors flock to Gamla Stan to experience attractions such as the royal palace, the daily changing of the guard, a number of old churches and many charming cafés and pubs in medieval vaults. If you take the ferry across to the adjacent island of Skeppsholmen, you'll discover modern museums and plenty of nature.

1 HildaHilda

Who could possibly resist Lott Hilde-brand's cheerful, naive designs? Her table runners, kitchen towels and oven-mitts decorated with egg, flower, fish and fruit motifs bring colour into the kitchen. Also very popular are cute little pouches for makeup, glasses or charger cables whose designs tell you what goes inside. HildaHilda products bring a smile to your face and are made with a lot of love. The designer developed a special weaving technique for her slightly coarse organic cotton and linen fabrics, and all products are made in Sweden.

Österlånggatan 21
www.hildahilda.se

2 M17

M17, where the ingenious confectioner Josefin Emteryd runs a café cum design store at a prime location on Mälartorget square, is the polar opposite of the old town's established retail and food businesses. If you like rustic furniture and home accessories, you'll love the wine glasses made of recycled bottles, industrial-style lamps and vintage wooden chests. There's a fluid transition between the store and café, where Josefin serves delicious baked goods, excellent coffee, sandwiches and ice cream made by a regional organic dairy.

Mälartorget 17
www.butikm17.se

3 Cultur

Ignore the waiters trying to attract you to the overpriced köttbullar in their restaurants and head to this gastropub instead. Its delightfully authentic concept makes it an oasis among the touristy bustle in the street. This is where locals meet for an inexpensive after-work glass of bubbly, wine or beer during happy hour (Mon–Fri 4–7 pm). Or they stay late with friends and feast on the range of light dishes served here. The interior is stylishly cosy, with designer furniture, works of contemporary art on the walls and small, intimate spaces.

Österlånggatan 34
www.culturbar.se

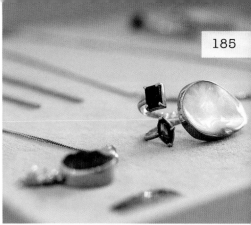

4 E. Torndahl

This store for everything beautiful has been in the same family since 1864. Founded by Ida Kunigunda Thorndal and passed on from mother to daughter, it's now run by great-great-granddaughter Lotta Imberg, who manages to stock sleek works by 70 Scandinavian designers in this small space. Her harmonious selection of contemporary Nordic designs ranges from jewellery and sunglasses to bags, stationery, cosmetics and children's fashion. A visit to this authentic jewel of a store in the old town is highly recommended.

Västerlånggatan 63
www.etorndahl.se

5 Kagges

A small restaurant with great ambition, whose young team serve first-rate modern Nordic cuisine with a lot of enthusiasm and energy. If you can, try to get a seat on the bar separating the open kitchen from the dining area so you can watch the staff cooking and plating up. In 2017, the daily newspaper *DN* recognised Kagges' unique combination of relaxed atmosphere and uncompromising quality with the highly coveted Gulddraken award for Stockholm's best mid-range restaurant.

Lilla Nygatan 21
www.kagges.com

Nordic light is much loved among artists.

6 Designfirman
Gamla Stan

Two shops by the Designfirman concept store, both located close to each other, offer lovingly curated selections of home accessories. Come here for pared-back and playful Nordic designs displayed side by side with all-Swedish objects such as elks and Dala horses. Animal and plant motifs are recurring themes, whether on cushion covers, prints, jewellery boxes or vases. Typically for stores in the old town, space is at a premium and it's therefore well worth visiting both stores if you don't want to miss anything.

Västerlånggatan 40 & 68
www.designfirman.com

Happy Socks®

Est. 2008 Sweden

7 Happy Socks

These cheerful socks, loved all over the world, come from Sweden, and are sold in a flagship store in Gamla Stan. If you take a close look at well-dressed locals, you'll notice that even gentlemen in suits love to wear these funky designs for a splash of colour in among their sophisticated grey, blue or black outfits. International comparisons have shown that Swedes place the greatest value on individuality and self-realisation – and Happy Socks allow them to express their character down to the tips of their toes.

Västerlånggatan 65
www.happysocks.com

8 Mister French

This waterside restaurant on Gamla Stan island is a mecca for fans of good seafood. Lobster, oysters and prawns are all fixtures on the menu, which is inspired by the cuisine of France's former colonies. Despite being quite large, the space retains a sophisticated lounge atmosphere. Dim lights, velvety sofas and armchairs, marble tables and Art Deco elements all create a luxurious vibe inside, while the open terrace has a Mediterranean air. On weekdays, the restaurant serves inexpensive lunches until 2:30 pm.

Skeppsbrokajen 103
www.mrfrench.se

9 Lena M

The pink umbrella in the shop window indicates that Lena M's small store and studio are open. This artist loves to include a few elk in her otherwise minimalist monochrome landscapes. She has also designed innumerable graphical patterns for postcards, trays and even cleaning cloths. Lena likes to showcase her art in a soothing environment with upcycled vintage furniture and a chilled playlist that hits the spot after you've been strolling through the busy laneways of the old town.

Kindstugatan 14
www.studiolenam.wordpress.com

Strong colours, elegant sculptures and pretty courtyards are typical of Stockholm's old town.

10 The Flying Elk

This gastropub at the edge of Gamla Stan is one of star chef Björn Frantzén's ventures. The Flying Elk is a very relaxed place, where British pub culture meets modern Swedish cuisine in a stylish, pared-down atmosphere. The namesake king of the Swedish forests is only found in paintings and sketches on the walls, though, and not on the menu, which instead features fish, steak, burgers and vegetarian dishes. Among the delicious desserts, Eton mess with strawberries and white chocolate is highly recommended.

Mälartorget 15
www.theflyingelk.se

11 Iris Hantverk

At first sight, Iris Hantverk looks like a friendly designer store. Situated among the tourist traps, this haven's authentic products are reason enough for a peek, but there's more behind this company, originally founded as a brush manufacturer in 1870. Brushmaking used to be a craft reserved for the blind, and Iris Hantverk still honours this custom. The store stocks not only handmade brushes, but also other useful kitchen, bathroom and garden accessories. Shop here to do yourself a favour and support a worthwhile endeavour.

Västerlånggatan 24
www.irishantverk.se

12 Pharmarium

This cocktail bar is well worth a visit, not only for its extravagant drinks menu, but also for its unusual interior. Sweden's first pharmacy opened here, at Stockholm's market square, in 1575, and the place is clearly still fascinated by ingredients at the intersection between medicine and magic. Innumerable small drawers and old-fashioned equipment will ignite your imagination while also forming an intriguing, chic background for a cocktail. Drinks are referred to as 'spirituosa', while 'substantia' means food.

Stortorget 7
www.pharmarium.se

13 Znogg

While the magic ingredient in Blå Gungan (p. 199) is a carefully measured dose of kitsch, this shop just a stone's throw away stocks accessories that make for subtler additions to your home. Very typically Swedish, the motifs on cups, plates and aprons are inspired by nature and the sea. The owners of the two stores say that, although they are theoretically in competition, they much prefer to enjoy their shared love of design and out-of-the-ordinary products as best friends. In fact their tastes are so different that there's essentially no overlap.

Österlånggatan 24
www.znogg.se

14 Moderna Museet

This gallery for art from 1900 onwards is worth a visit for a number of reasons. Firstly, there's the collection. With works by Matisse, Picasso, Olafur Eliasson and Andy Warhol, plus leading temporary exhibitions, it is renowned all over the world. Then there are about a dozen sculptures around the gallery, which can be admired at any time of the day or night. Entry to the gallery is free. Finally, the gallery restaurant has a fabulous view of Strandvägen boulevard, and tiny, peaceful Skeppsholmen island has beautiful walkways.

Exercisplan 4

www.modernamuseet.se

15 Blå Gungan

Once you've made it past touristy Väster-långgatan and across Järntorget square, it's time to relax. Ahead of you lies the much quieter Österlånggatan lane with its authentic stores and restaurants. Blå Gungan is an excellent address for unusual souvenirs and original design products, with many products in the range being by local designers. The tableware designed by illustrator Ingela P. Arrhenius, who lives only a few steps away in Gamla Stan, is particularly popular. Its colourful motifs include faces, cities and animals.

Österlånggatan 16
www.blagungan.se

KIERAN LONG

Gallery director with a passion for
architecture and design

BRIT KIERAN LONG IS AN EMINENT AUTHORITY on the modern architecture and design scene. A former journalist and architecture critic, he has also hosted reality TV shows such as *Restoration Home* on the BBC, taking viewers on-site to witness spectacular home renovations. In 2013, he moved from media to galleries and established the design department at London's Victoria & Albert Museum. He took over as director of the ArkDes Centre for Architecture and Design in Stockholm in 2017.

You're originally from London. What do you find fascinating about Stockholm?

Something that's quite special about Stockholm is that it is a European city that is very much preserved – Sweden was never bombed or a theatre of war. As a Londoner I find it most surprising to see just how many historical eras are evident in Stockholm's city centre side by side.

Which buildings do you find most impressive?

The Stockholm Public Library by Gunnar Asplund is an important building in the world history of architecture. It is a thoroughly beautiful, fascinating and playful building that was constructed just before the emergence of modernism. From there, you can walk to Riksförsäkringsanstalten, a rational office building for an insurance, which was designed by famous architect Sigurd Lewerentz and built in the 1930s. I also like the Konserthuset, where the Nobel Prize ceremony is held. This elegant, almost classicist concert house by Ivar Tengbom opened in 1926. I suggest you end your architectural walk at Kulturhuset, a modernist building by Peter Celsing from the late 1960s.

How do architecture and design fit together?

We at the ArkDes Centre think that everything, from the way a city is planned through to the design of a smartphone, creates public relationships between people. On the one hand, a large part of life takes place within a city's public realm, where we have coffee, go to vote, demonstrate and raise our children. But we also spend a lot of time in digital worlds, which are also underpinned by design. That's why we at ArkDes want to examine all types and forms of design and elicit just how they impact on the lives of today's citizens.

Which part of the Centre deserves particular attention?

The permanent exhibition gives an overview of the history of Swedish architecture. People should definitely go and see the 3D models of hundreds of very different buildings. For example, there's a model of Katarinahissen, a 19th-century public elevator that used to carry people up the cliffs of Södermalm island. And there are examples of Swedish modernism. My favourite among these is the Luma factory, which still manufactures light bulbs even today. The factory was designed by Kooperativa förbundets arkitektkontor, an influential architectural practice at its time. We know that the French architect Le Corbusier visited the Luma factory and was inspired by it.

What's your vision for the museum?
I'd like to turn ArkDes into a place of extraordinary creativity. This applies to both of its traditional thematic fields of architecture and design, which we have in our collection and for which Sweden is renowned. I want to add new fields of design to this discourse; fields that are just emerging all over the world thanks to new technology, from fan art to video games and biological design. All of these fields will sooner or later engage in a dialogue with the more traditional aspects of design. There has already been one major change. In 2018, we opened a new gallery named Boxen by Dehlin Brattgård, a young architectural practice. I'm proud that we also have a piece of modern architecture in the Centre instead of just models.

Do you have a lot of Swedish design objects in your home?
I sure do! I'm married to the Swedish product designer Sofia Lagerkvist, so we have a lot of designs by her studio, Front, at home, from lamps through to carpets. What I love about Sweden is that high-quality design forms part of everyday life. It doesn't matter where you go: the drinking glasses will have been carefully selected and the typography will be stylish. In Stockholm, the understanding of design goes so deep that you're always surrounded by it.

Gamla Stan is just a short ferry trip away. Do you like spending time in the old town?
Definitely. Gamla Stan is a marvellously well-preserved urban structure from the Middle Ages. Of course, there are a lot of tourists, but plenty of 'normal' people are moving back into the old town. You could say that it is being recolonised by locals.

Where should people visit in Gamla Stan?
I highly recommend a stroll from the royal palace to Stortorget square. You might notice that the city's main church, Storkyrkan, is not directly on the square, in contrast to most European cities. This is because Stockholm was originally established as a trading centre, and that's something I still feel today: people can be a bit reserved, but they love business.

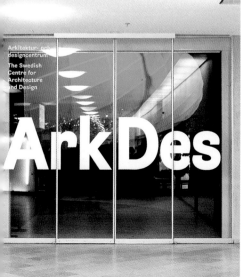

16 ArkDes

The Swedish Centre for Architecture and Design is associated with the Moderne Museet gallery, and entry is also free. The Centre is a lot smaller and has one or two special exhibitions as well as a permanent exhibition, where 3D models illustrate the development of Swedish architecture. The light and airy library with a glass front and park view is open to all visitors. Its collection of architecture and design books and magazines also features some titles in other languages, including English.

Exercisplan 4

www.arkdes.se

No cars, but quiet, atmospheric little lanes: Stockholm's charming old town.

The huge Vasaparken city park offers plenty of space for relaxation, fun and games.

COFFEE AND ART:
VASASTAN

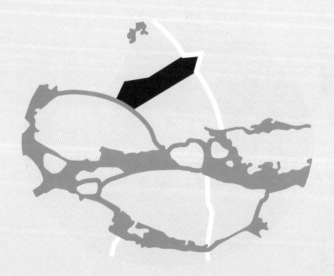

Quiet residential area or the city's beating heart? With its retro charm and expansive city park, the up-and-coming suburb of Vasastan is a favourite for people who want to explore Stockholm beyond the inner-city bustle. This is where you can feel like a true local. If you want to indulge in a proper Swedish *fika*, the best place to go is one of the cafés near Stockholm's famous public library, where you'll be treated to lovingly brewed coffee from local micro-roasters. Vasastan is also a hotspot for finding rare treasures, and browsing the antiques stores along Upplandsgatan street on Saturdays is an authentic part of Stockholm shopping culture.

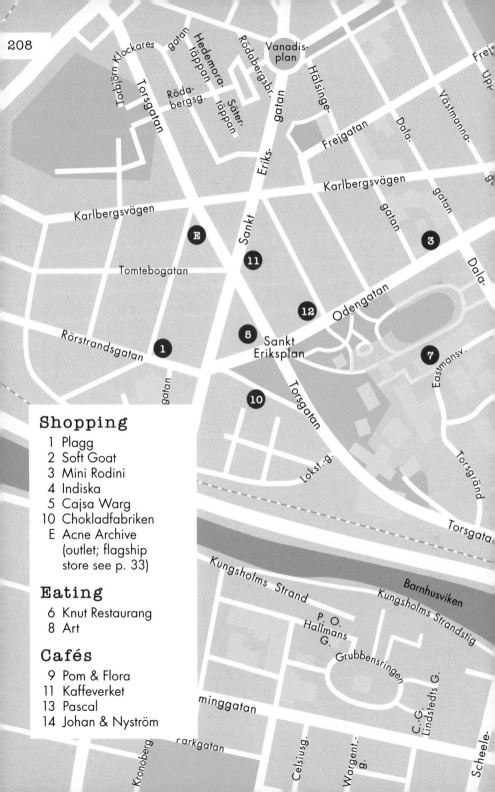

Shopping

1 Plagg
2 Soft Goat
3 Mini Rodini
4 Indiska
5 Cajsa Warg
10 Chokladfabriken
E Acne Archive
   (outlet; flagship
   store see p. 33)

Eating

6 Knut Restaurang
8 Art

Cafés

9 Pom & Flora
11 Kaffeverket
13 Pascal
14 Johan & Nyström

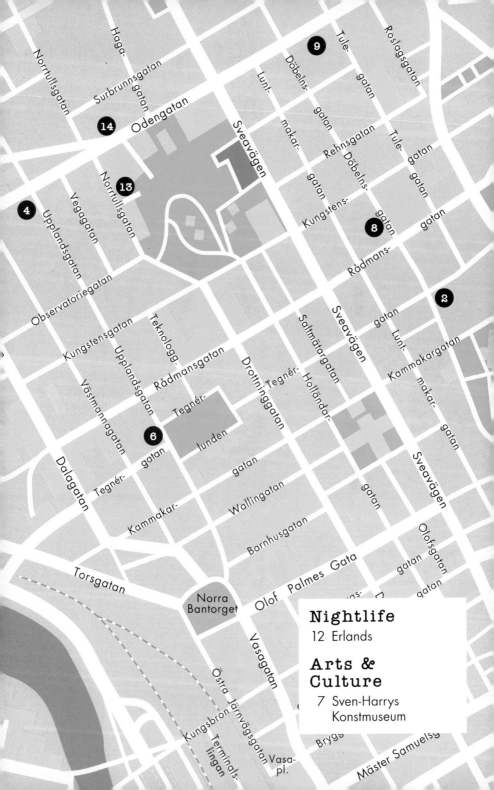

Nightlife
12 Erlands

Arts & Culture
7 Sven-Harrys Konstmuseum

1 Plagg

This fashion boutique stocks a good range of Scandinavian labels to dress women and men in style from top to toe. It specialises not so much in ephemeral fashion as in classic pieces for a wardrobe that'll last. It is located in Rörstrandsgatan street, also known as Stockholm's 'Little Paris', as it is lined with cafés and restaurants where you can sit outside in summer. Also in summer, the street is blocked off for cars for a couple of months so that locals and visitors can enjoy their shopping and *fika* experience even more.

Rörstrandsgatan 8
www.plagg.se

2 Soft Goat

Did you know that it takes two to four years for the hair of a cashmere goat to grow long enough for spinning it into wool? Soft Goat specialises in exclusive products made out of 100 per cent cashmere. The store stocks both fashion pieces and timeless classics for women and men. The label's two annual collections show that cashmere can in fact be worn year round: lightweight short-sleeved models in cheerful colours make a great addition to your summer wardrobe.

Tegnérgatan 13
www.softgoat.com

3 Mini Rodini

This Stockholm childrenswear brand is renowned for imaginative prints and practical designs. Its concept was developed by illustrator Cassandra Rhodin, who wanted to make it easy for parents to dress their children in comfortable, fairly produced shirts and trousers. The ideals of sustainability and healthy eating are integrated into playful motifs and designs, with funky prints reading 'We must protect Mother Earth' or 'Eat more vegetables'. The label also has an outlet store, Treasures (Hornsgatan 71, see map p. 148, C). Odengatan 78
www.minirodini.com

4 Indiska

If H&M had been invented in India, this is probably what it would look like. This venture, which started in 1901 as an exhibition of laboriously imported exotic artefacts and an Indian man smoking a shisha, is now a successful chainstore selling inexpensive, colourful fashion and home accessories right in the heart of Stockholm. The print dresses bring at least an illusion of warmth to the cool Nordic climate. And because Indiska is still a Swedish label, its designers subscribe to the Scandinavian motto of classic cuts that simply fit well.

Odengatan 79
www.indiska.com

FÄBODKNÄCKE 47⁹⁰ /st

SPISBRÖD 52⁹⁰ st

5 Cajsa Warg

This market deli stocks Swedish and international specialty foods for gourmets in tall wooden shelves accessed via ladders. Shop for crispbread and indulge in a foodie dream come true to a background of classical music. Put together a very special picnic from the hand-picked range or stock up on edible souvenirs. The store is named after a well-known 18th-century Swedish cookbook author, whose *Guide to Housekeeping for Young Women* was even translated into German and Estonian.
Sankt Eriksplan 2
www.cajsawarg.se

6 Knut Restaurang

This rustic-cool restaurant serves Swedish cuisine with all the trimmings: herring, elk, reindeer, salmon, caviar and cloud-berries. Worn wooden tables, a mix of chairs and antler decorations on the walls only strengthen the impression that you've been transported far from the city to a town of reindeer breeders in northern Lapland. If you want to get a sense of authentic Nordic cuisine and explore out-of-the-ordinary dishes and cocktails, this is the place for you. The restaurant's inexpensive lunches are popular among local workers.

Upplandsgatan 17
www.restaurangknut.se

7 Sven-Harrys Konstmuseum

A magnificent building at the edge of Vasaparken is home to a very special art gallery. The ground floor is a venue for regularly changing exhibitions, but the highlight is on the roof, where the apartment of gallery founder Sven-Harry Karlsson has been replicated with all of its designer furniture and paintings. The apartment is only accessible with a guided tour, usually available several times a day from Wednesday to Sunday. Tours end on the roof terrace, from where you get a great view across Vasastan. Eastmansvägen 10
www.sven-harrys.se

8 Art

A restaurant experience for insiders. Once you pass through the painted front door and ask to be let in from the phone booth right behind it, you'll find yourself in a dimly lit restaurant with windowless, graffiti-covered walls and relaxed staff. In this unusual atmosphere, diners are served several mid-sized courses at a pleasant pace. You can eat à la carte or allow yourself to be surprised by the six-course menu. The food is excellent, and you'll probably be only too happy to stay on for another glass of wine or a cocktail.
Döbelnsgatan 45
www.restaurangart.se

9 Pom & Flora

This café is famous for its breakfast bowls, which are lovingly prepared and go well beyond standard muesli fare. Chia pudding may already have found a broad following, but Pom & Flora's combinations with smoothies, peanut butter, dates, tahini or pollen might inspire you to take it to the next level in your own kitchen. And it's good news for people who like to sleep in: breakfast is available all day. The café also serves sweet bites such as brioche with rhubarb jam and toasted sandwiches with inspired fillings.
Odengatan 39
www.pomochflora.se

10 Chokladfabriken

Don't even try to stick to healthy in here. These handmade chocolates, tarts and tartlets are Stockholm's first choice for sweet gifts. Chocolate bars with well-known Swedish designs on both the wrappers and chocolates make a great souvenir for design fans back at home. Adventurous gourmets may want to try creations made out of chocolate, licorice and sea salt. The Vasastan store is closed on Sundays, but at the Södermalm branch (Renstiernasgata 12) you can get your sweet fix seven days a week.
St. Eriksplan 9
www.chokladfabriken.com

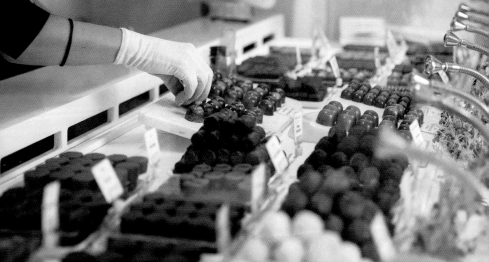

11 Kaffeverket

Kaffeverket, a hip café on St. Eriksplan square, is a treat for both the eye and palate. Its interior with grey-green wood panels and white tiles features regularly on Instagram, and its culinary offerings definitely live up to its high visual standard. Some come for the perfectly roasted coffee, others for the selection of delicious and healthy dishes written on the blackboard above the counter. The toasted banana bread with honey and mascarpone makes for a great alternative to cinnamon scrolls, and the Asian-inspired salads reliably hit the spot at lunchtime.
Sankt Eriksgatan 88
www.kaffeverket.nu

12 Erlands

This tiny bar in a side street off Odengatan is like a delightful time capsule
from the 1950s and 1960s. The guys
behind the counter wear bow ties, waist-
coats and hats, and the soundtrack is
period jazz. Locals and tourists alike
flock to the bar for its cocktails and
idiosyncratic ambience. The drinks menu
changes every two weeks – only the
house drink 'Erlands', a martini with
elderflower notes, is always available.
Sit down at one of the cosy window
tables or retreat to the delightful
loungeroom upstairs.
Gästrikegatan 1
www.erlandsbar.se

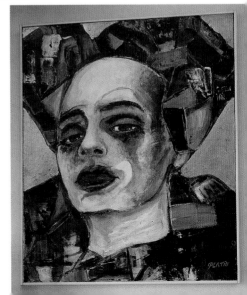

13 Pascal

This popular hipster café near the Stockholm public library is run by three siblings with a passion for coffee. The coffee beans come from Swedish micro-roasters, the cinnamon scrolls are made by Pascal's own bakery, and hot dishes are prepared fresh. All this deliciousness comes in a space fitted out in a typically Nordic minimalist design. Coarsely rendered walls, simple wooden furniture, sleek lamps and lots of pot plants have made Pascal's a firm favourite on Instagram.
Norrtullsgatan 4
www.cafepascal.se

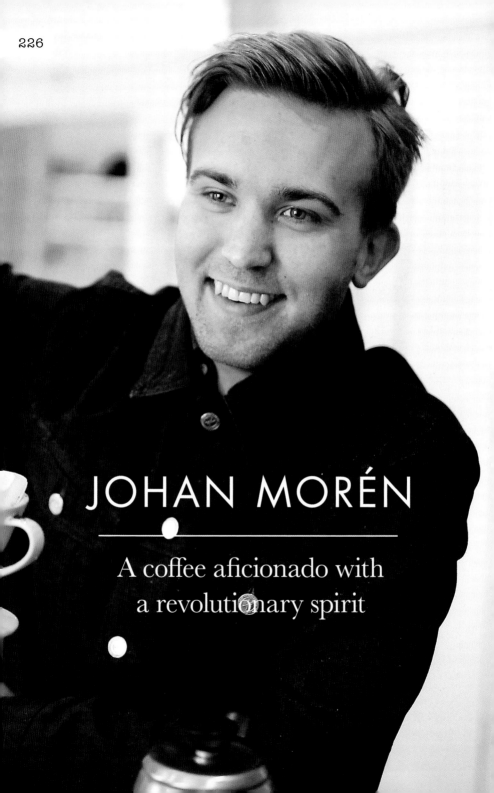

JOHAN MORÉN

A coffee aficionado with
a revolutionary spirit

JOHAN MORÉN has been managing director of Stockholm coffee brand Johan & Nyström since 2018, when the company opened its fourth café in Vasastan, serving specialties from its own coffee roasters. Johan & Nyström's baristas use a range of techniques to get the best out of their coffees. In our interview, Johan explains the phenomenon of sociable coffee breaks, lifts the secret of good coffee and shares an insider's perspective of the Stockholm coffee scene.

How would you explain the concept of *fika* to a non-Swede?

The word was created by switching around the syllables of the old word for coffee (*kaffi*). But *fika* has become so much more than a cup of coffee – it's become a Swedish institution. It's still fundamentally the same thing as ever: a cup of coffee with a little bite to eat, often a cinnamon scroll. But the social context is much more important. For example, at work everybody gets together in the kitchen at some time between 10 am and 2 pm to have a *fika* and a chat, whether about the meaning of life, work or your last holiday. Talking is more important than what's on the table. Also, *fika* has come to be time away from screens. You spend time together, relax and talk face to face.

What's special about coffee by Johan & Nyström?

Our strength is that we're responsible for the entire process. We often travel to meet our producers directly, and we know every single step, from the plant to the cup. This is how we make sure we only work with pros! Johan & Nyström stands for committed people and consistent values.

What's the secret of really good coffee?

For me, it's the entire value chain. Good coffee starts with a producer who harvests the coffee fruit when it is perfectly ripe. Roasters process the beans. If they don't know what they're doing, the producer's good work was for nothing. And the last person in the value chain is the barista, who uses the right techniques and technology to get the best out of the coffee. But it's not only about high-quality coffee. You also need the right environment – a clean, well-designed café where guests can explore different flavours and aromas, all of which tell stories about where the coffee originated.

How was Johan & Nyström established?

Johan & Nyström was founded as a coffee roaster in Stockholm in 2004. At the time, coffee was really boring in Sweden. The only options were medium or dark roast. We wanted to start a coffee revolution. That's still our slogan even today, and it means that we create more coffee choice and offer different flavours. At first, we sold our roasted beans to cafés and restaurants across Sweden, but then we wanted to increase our visibility and opened our own café and store at Mariatorget square on Södermalm to show people how good coffee can actually taste! The interest in specialty coffees has grown more and more, and we now have ten cafés in Sweden and Finland. And they're not only in trendy suburbs, but also at airports and in city centres. Because good coffee is something for everybody, not just for hipsters.

What's happening in the Stockholm coffee scene?

High-quality beans and specialty coffees from good roasters have become standard in many cafés and restaurants. It's become trendy to experiment with a range of beverages and flavours, for example matcha latte or mixtures with activated charcoal or beetroot. For summer, there are also new cold coffee beverages. Cold brew, that is coffee prepared with cold water, is the latest big trend. I hope that new flavours and techniques will bring a new wave of energy into coffee culture.

Why did you choose Vasastan as your location?

Johan & Nyström was very well established on trendy Södermalm, but for me that wasn't enough. There are also plenty of well-informed, curious consumers here in Vasastan, and they want to explore more. They care about where their food comes from, and that's a good fit for our brand. Also Odenplan square has become a bit of a hub since the new train station was opened in 2017 – almost every commuter passes through here. It's the right spot for taking our coffee revolution further.

What sort of atmosphere do you want to create in your café?

I describe our design theme as 'modern craft'. We want to create an artisan atmosphere, because for me that's what the production and preparation of coffee is. The ripped wallpaper and visible bare walls behind have something raw. Finally, our processes must be efficient, so that guests don't have to wait.

What are your must-see places for visitors to Vasastan?

Lilla Ego (Västmannagatan 69) is my absolutely favourite restaurant. Again, this is a place with a bit of a raw interior, with unrendered brick walls. The two chefs cook fantastic food. It's a great combination of corner restaurant and fine dining.

KAFFEREVOLUTION

14 Johan & Nyström

The vision of this coffee roaster, founded in Stockholm in 2004, is to make sustainably produced, expertly prepared specialty coffees accessible – a minor revolution in a country where stale filter coffee tends to be the norm. No longer is an appreciation of delicate aromas in carefully brewed coffee the prerogative of aficionados – Johan & Nyström cafés invite everybody to discover new aspects of coffee. The attached store sells coffee beans, tea in pretty tins, pots and all sorts of equipment for enjoying coffee at home.

Odengatan 62
www.johanochnystrom.se

*Recently renovated Odenplan
square is the gate to Vasastan.*

Most visitors don't explore
Kungsholmen island beyond
Stockholm's landmark
Stadshuset city hall.
Are you curious to see more?

THE BEST SPOTS ON THE WATER:
KUNGSHOLMEN

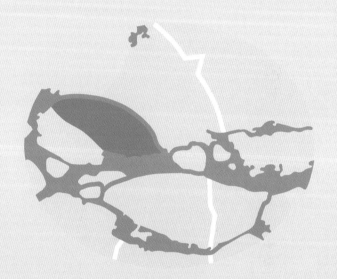

Kungsholmen's attractions include authentic waterfront cafés and restaurants and lovely parklands around the entire island. Walking the island circuit only takes about 90 minutes, and you'll traverse parks from eleven centuries, from the national Romanticist nature reserve in the east to the hypermodern landscaping in the west. Hornsbergs Strandpark is Stockholm's summer playground, where people come to swim, barbecue, party and promenade. The architecture is dominated by glass office buildings, modern residential blocks and three-storey houses in the functionalist style of the 1930s. Stockholm's landmark town hall is at the eastern end of the island.

Rörstrands-

Norrbacka-

Birkagatan

gatan

Klarastrandsleden

Karlbergssjön

Kungsholms

gatan

Svarvar-

Alströmergatan

gatan

Flemminggatan

8

Sankt

Arbetar-

Göransgatan

Bergs-

nsvägen

Fridhems-
plan

Sysslomansgatan

Fridhemsgatan

Karlsviksgatan

Sankt Eriksgatan

Norr Mälarstrand

hovsleden

7

vägen

Norr

Mälarstrand

Sankt Eriksplan

Odengatan

Eastmansv.

Olivecronasv.

Atlasgatan

Torsgatan

Torsgränd

Atlasmuren

S:t Eriks-
bron

Strand

Kungsholms Strandstig

Barnhusviken

Fridhemsgatan

Eriksgatan

gatan

Inedalsgatan

Grubbens
G.

Grubbensringen

Sankt

Kronobergs-

Parkgatan

Fleminggatan

gatan

gatan

gatan

Kungsholms-

Norra Agnegatan

gatan

5

Hantverkargatan

Bergs-

Scheele-

9

B. von Platens G.

Sankt Ponton-

järgatan

Polhems-

J. Erics-

sonsgatan

Pilgatan

S. Agnegatan

Hantverkargatan

gatan

Pipers-

Kungsholmstorg

Garvargatan

4

1

6

Västerbron

1 Norrmälarstrands Blommor

This florist is preserving a piece of Eden across a few square metres of retail space. Flower arrangements in the window invite passers-by to come in, where they find a large selection of cut flowers and pot plants. The most exquisite flowers are displayed behind glass, like precious jewels. A look inside is worthwhile, even if you don't live in Stockholm. You're bound to find the arrangements inspiring, and the flower pots and garden accessories are very portable.

Norr Mälarstrand 30
www.norrmalarstrandsblommor.se

2 Fryst

This inconspicuous ice creamery on Kungsholmen's northern promenade sells what many believe to be Stockholm's best gelato – plus it has a fabulous view of Karlberg Palace. Flavours including rhubarb and cardamom, and strawberry and lime, provide plenty of variety without ever going over the top. Fryst, a family business managed by mother Rehné and son Kim, is usually open from Wednesday to Sunday 12–6 pm. Don't be scared off if there seems to be a long queue: the staff are very professional and serve customers quickly.

Kungsholms Strand 167
www.fryst.net

3 Piren

In the summer, many Swedes like to get out of the city. Those who stay often enjoy a little break at Piren, a waterside restaurant with a large covered terrace that is the perfect spot for relaxing, eating mussels or fish soup and watching the sunset. From May to September, the restaurant hosts DJs on Wednesday to Saturday nights, who turn it into a little piece of Nordic Ibiza. If you visit on a cool day, inside has a modern yet cosy atmosphere with an open fireplace.
Kristinebergs Strand 2
www.piren-bar.se

4 Mälarpaviljongen

This oasis in the heart of Stockholm is where you should head if you feel like healthy food and a cool glass of beer or bubbly and want to explore Nordic home accessories at the same time. Enjoy the outdoor space in the garden or mingle with locals at the bar, which is built on a pontoon right above the water. The view of Riddarfjärden bay and the neighbouring island of Södermalm is amazing, as is the atmosphere among the diverse group of patrons. The attached design shop stocks accessories for gardens and balconies. Open from mid-April to September.
Norr Mälarstrand 64
www.malarpaviljongen.se

TUNACADO
Tonfiskmousse, Avokado,
Tomat, Pesto
403 kcal

SERRANO
Serranoskinka, Mozzarella, Avokado,
Tomat, Pesto
389 kcal

JOE'S CLUB
Kyckling, Avokado,
Tomat, Pesto
471 kcal

SPICY TUNA
Tonfiskmousse, Jalapeños, Tabasco,
Tomat, Pesto
417 kcal

THE COLD ONES...
Small (12 oz) / Large (16 oz)

ICE LATTE
147 / 209 kcal
38 / 42

ICE AMERICANO
7 kcal
28 / 32

COFFEE SHAKE
Espresso shot, Vaniljmjölk
188 / 249 kcal
50 / 62

ORGANISK

5 Joe & The Juice

This Danish chain of hip juice bars has taken not only Norway, the USA and the UK, but also Sweden by storm. There are about 30 branches in Stockholm alone, including the one on Kungsholmen. Top up your vitamin levels with freshly prepared juices, shakes and fruit shots, and fill up on muffins and sandwiches. They also do good coffee. It's no secret, and possibly part of the attraction, that the baristas (or 'juicers' as they're called here) are only young, good-looking males.

Scheelegatan 9
www.joejuice.com

6 Orangeriet

One of Stockholm's most beautiful bars is right on the Norr Mälarstrand waterfront promenade with a view of Riddarfjärden bay, the western corner of Södermalm and the green island of Långholmen. As you relax next to the fireplace inside, you could be forgiven for thinking you're in a Mediterranean country home. With its rattan furniture and lemon trees, the space offers a unique ambience at any time of the year. The menu is Italian, from antipasti to pizza and sweets. The bar serves refreshing cocktails, and there are regular guest appearances by DJs.

Norr Mälarstrand 464
www.orangerietbar.se

7 Rålambshovsparken & Boulebar

How about a bit of good food, fresh air and exercise? During the warmer months, the Boulebar in Rålambshovsparken is a popular destination for Stockholmers who want to test their boules skills in the fresh air. Naturally, the kitchen serves southern French cuisine, but if you're after something different, you can get delicious light meals from one of the food trucks along Rålambshovsleden street until 9 pm. Walk along the park and under Västerbron bridge to reach Smedsuddsbadet beach, where you can swim.

Smedsuddsvägen 2
www.boulebar.se

8 Haga Tårtcompani & Bageri

As unassuming as this café might look, it serves a huge range of sweet temptations, all made by the in-house patisserie, including cinnamon scrolls, fruit tarts and exquisite desserts, but also great sandwiches. Oscar Målevik and Anna Cardelius are conventionally trained pastry chefs, but like to add a contemporary touch to their creations. When Lady Gaga toured Stockholm in 2015, her team ordered a custom chocolate cake from Haga, which is still available upon special order.

Fleminggatan 107
www.hagabageri.se

9 Amaranten

This boutique hotel is centrally located only about ten minutes' walk from the central train and bus station, but it's quieter than many comparable places on Norrmalm or Södermalm. Amaranten has 461 glamorous and generously sized rooms decorated in 1960s style. After an eventful day, guests can relax in the in-house sauna, enjoy a drink at the cocktail bar or indulge in the culinary creations of star chef Marcus Samuelsson, who fuses the very best of Kungsholmen and Manhattan in the hotel restaurant, Kitchen & Table.

Kungsholmsgatan 31
www.nordicchoicehotels.se

BENGT ISLING

An ingenious
landscape architect

BENGT ISLING'S WORK AS A LANDSCAPE ARCHITECT with the Nyréns architectural practice has been awarded more prizes than that of any other Swede. His masterpiece is Hornsbergs Strandpark in the west of Kungsholmen island, a well thought-out urban oasis that attracts visitors from all over Stockholm to its promenades, picnic spots and swimming beaches. In this interview, Bengt shares insights into Stockholm's green heart.

What makes Hornsbergs Strandpark so unique?
As with all of my projects, I wanted to make full use of the local environment and conditions. Hornsberg is in the west of the island and therefore gets the evening sun. On warm summer nights, when the sun shines until 10 pm, the place is full of people from all over the city. There's nowhere else in the inner city where you can be in a park so close to the water and watch the sun set.

You were awarded the Swedish architectural association's Siena Prize for Hornsbergs Strandpark in 2012. Why has your design been so successful?
The park feels very much like a public place and therefore attracts people from other parts of town. It's not only for people who live locally. We achieved this by having a narrow street separating the park from adjacent built-up spaces, which gives the place an urban character. This allows visitors and local residents to share the space very closely without being in each other's way. There's also a wall to separate the park and the street and make the space safer, as children can't run onto the street. You are very close to the city, feel safe and can fully enjoy being outdoors. Everything is thought through.

As you stroll through the park along the water, you keep discovering little details everywhere. Would you describe the park as being interactive?
Definitely. The benches are aligned to catch the sun, wooden walkways allow you to get close to the water, and if you want to go for a swim, there are a number of ladders down to the water. Plus there are lots and lots of design elements: a pergola, showers and floating islands with built-in BBQs. Everything shares a uniform, robust language of form that is expressed in wood and weathered metal.

How would you describe the style of the park?
You feel very clearly that it is made by humans in a design that has international calibre. I never wanted visitors to feel as if they're walking through preserved nature; I wanted them to know that this is a park. That's why we only included meticulously placed exotic plants,

among them bald cypresses and birch trees from the Himalayas. If you walk through older parks such as the one on Norr Mälarstrand street here on Kungsholmen, you might think it's a piece of forgotten nature. That's the national Romanticist style, where everything was intentionally as natural and Swedish-looking as possible. Sven Hermelin, the father of Swedish landscape architecture, once said, 'If people don't notice I've been at work, then I've done my work well'. I'd say the exact opposite.

And how long did it take from the idea to the finished park?
Ten years. It can be tiring when projects take such a long time. But in the end I'm always happy to see my ideas becoming reality. That's one of the reasons why I've never changed careers. If you start a project, you want to see it through, otherwise somebody else will reap the rewards.

What does designing parks mean for you?
My wife always says that I'm the world's most cheerful landscape architect. My work means a lot to me. The entire process from the idea to the first sketches and plans through to the construction process is fascinating. If I then visit a few years later, I see not only how the idea has been put into practice, but also that it makes other people happy. You actually change a visible and tangible element of the city, perhaps for centuries to come. That's a feeling that's hard to beat.

What is your association with Kungsholmen?
This part of Stockholm is a fixture in my daily work. It's where the city's town and landscape planning department is located, which I attend several times a week, as they're a major client of mine. I also often walk through the parks along Norr Mälarstrand and the Stadshuset town hall, which I find very inspiring. For me, they're two shining examples of landscape architecture. And I got married at the Stadshuset. It's a fantastic place with an open courtyard, lovely arcades and, of course, the magnificent park.

Which other parks should visitors see while in Stockholm?
For something very different from Hornsberg, I suggest Hagaparken, a 250-year-old park in the English style. When compared to other parks worldwide, it might not be anything extraordinary, but it's huge and has lots of water and nature. You can walk forever and just keep discovering new cultural sights, as the park once surrounded the royal residence, and the king had a number of small pavilions built all over the place. Today, Princess Victoria lives in the palace, which you can see as you stroll past. It's a unique place where culture meets nature.

10 Hornsbergs Strandpark

The waterfront promenade along the western side of Kungsholmen is a much-loved place for BBQs and picnics. Nyréns architects really thought of everything when designing this park: there are ladders down to the water, curved wooden walkways for walking and three floating islands. The concept of an urban oasis where the city meets the water in the midst of generous green spaces was awarded the distinguished Siena Prize for landscape architecture in 2012. The food options in the park range from pizza to gourmet kebabs and vegetarian burgers.

Hornsbergs Strand 47

The park along Norr Mälar-
strand invites you to slow down.

Lökholms-
hålet

Sandhamnssundet

Trovillevägen

Trovillevägen

Trovillevägen

Trovillevägen

Trovillevägen

Trovillevägen

Shopping
2 Sommarboden
5 Sea Life

Eating
3 Sandhamns Värdshus

Cafés
4 Sandhamns Bageri
6 Strindbergsgården

Hotel
1 Seglarhotell

AN ISLAND AT THE
OUTER ARCHIPELAGO:
SANDHAMN

Missing out on the Stockholm archipelago means missing out on a piece of the city's identity. The Baltic coast off Stockholm is dotted with about 30,000 islands, some of which are home to entire villages. This is where Swedish design enters a new dimension in the form of small, maritime-themed fashion and accessory boutiques, stylish hotels and exciting art. One of the most popular islands is Sandhamn, where thousands of Stockholmers retreat for the summer. The Cinderella ferry from Strandvägen takes you to the island in only about two hours' time, and both the magical ferry ride through the archipelago and the unique flair, beaches and nature once you get there more than justify a day trip.

Princess of the archipelago: the Cinderella ferries take you straight from the city centre to Sandhamn.

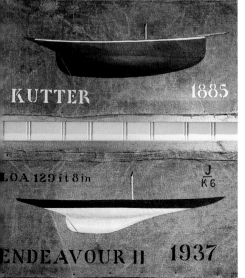

1 Seglarhotell

This hotel with its red façade and striking turret above the harbour of Sandhamn is more than mere accommodation: it's the island's social hub. This is where sailors relax with 'after sail' drinks and live music on Saturday afternoons, where you fortify yourself with a hearty pizza in the lounge, and where everybody who doesn't have their own boat stays. The restaurant on the first floor serves international cuisine and cocktails in an elegant atmosphere with breathtaking views of the sea.

www.sandhamn.com

2 Sommarboden

'I'm one of the crazy people who live on Sandhamn all year,' says Ann-Kathrin Öberg with a smile. Her store, probably the single most popular boutique in the entire archipelago, is open on weekends only between autumn and spring, but every day throughout the summer. She stocks relaxed maritime-styled fashion for both women and men. The menswear department is worth seeing, if only for the nautical interior lovingly hand-built by Ann-Kathrin's husband. ou can't miss this store: it's right on the harbour, and a table stacked with outfits in a marine look invite you to browse.

Popular summer residences: Sandhamn's colourful villas are where well-off Stockholmers love to spend their summers.

3 Sandhamns Värdshus

Sandhamn's top address for all matters culinary is only a few steps north of the harbour. The atmosphere on the ground floor is down-to-earth, while the first floor is more elegant, with paintings, nautical details, white tablecloths and plenty of room for families and groups. Ask for a table by the window, where you'll get a magnificent view across the bay. World-renowned crime author Viveca Sten has her summer house nearby and often comes to Sandhamns Värdshus for the fish soup. The restaurant is open year-round, but it's recommended to check the website before visiting off-season.
www.sandhamns-vardshus.se

4 Sandhamns Bageri

This small bakery next to the restaurant has supplied islanders and visitors with homemade cinnamon and cardamom scrolls, vanilla custard-filled *Wienerbröd*, sweet pretzels and Sandhamn's specialty pastry, sailors' buns (also sweet, of course), for decades. Take your coffee and sit down on one of the white outside tables if you'd like to meet some locals. The island is small and the mood is friendly to exuberant, especially in summer. Don't come too late in the day: in summer, the famous *bullar* are often sold out an hour before the bakery closes.

5 Sea Life

Between the harbour and the Seglar-hotell, you'll pass a row of small, red buildings, where you'll find a number of interesting shops. Sea Life fits out sailors and lovers of the marine look with stylish yet functional clothes, including the windproof quilted jackets in navy blue, beige and pink that everybody in the archipelago seems to wear. The store also sells home accessories with marine motifs such as sailor knots and light-houses. Whether you discover your inner sailor on Sandhamn or are only looking for a keepsake of its sea breeze, you're bound to find your perfect souvenir here. www.sealife.se

6 Strindbergsgården

This picturesque garden café is Sand-hamn's idyllic oasis for sunny days and the perfect place for a classic Swedish *fika*, a social break over a cup of coffee and a sweet pastry, in the fresh island air. Water and harbour views are included. You can also stay overnight in the attached guesthouse, a red wooden building with a history of over 100 years. Its guests have included royals and famous visitors such as playwright August Strindberg and tennis pro Björn Borg. The interior is well preserved and makes for an unforgettable stay.

www.strindbergsgarden.com

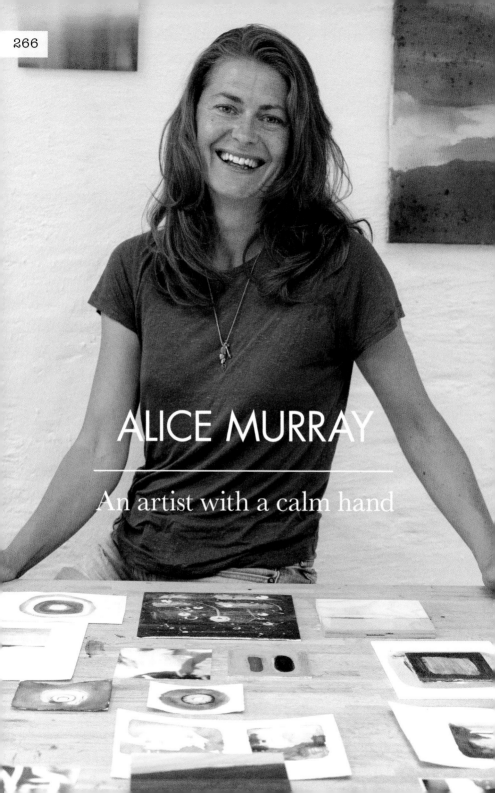

ALICE MURRAY

An artist with a calm hand

HAVING STUDIED FINE ARTS IN AMSTERDAM, artist Alice Murray returned to her home town of Stockholm ten years ago. Most of the year she works in her private studio, which visitors are only given access to for the once-yearly open day. For Alice, summers on Sandhamn are the highlight of the year. She finds serenity and inspiration at her family's holiday home and sometimes – depending on her creative flow – even sells works here that are inspired by the natural environment of the Swedish archipelago.

What is your association with Sandhamn?

I essentially grew up on Sandhamn. My parents bought this holiday house just before I was born. I was two weeks old on my first visit, and I've spent every single summer there ever since. Sandhamn is my summer home and my own place in the midst of nature, right on the sea. I grew up with a view of the horizon, because you don't see any other islands from our house. Whenever I sit there in the shade, I'm deeply happy. The light and sounds can evoke any number of childhood memories.

What does Sandhamn mean for you as an artist?

A few years ago I went through a phase when I painted a lot of miniatures of Sandhamn motifs. During the summer, I'd sit in the garden of my sister's summer home, hang paintings from the trees and put out a handwritten 'Art for Sale' sign. My paintings never sold as quickly as they did then. Naturalist Sandhamn motifs featuring the forest, the beach and the interplay between light and shadow are essentially my bestsellers. But I can't paint them on demand. There have been years without me painting even a single one.

Where can people see your art?

In recent years, I've had exhibitions in the Stockholm old town and on Sandhamn as well as one in Barcelona. I'm still building contacts to galleries in Stockholm and am hoping to have regular exhibitions organised. My homepage and Instagram feed showcase my works to the entire world.

How would you describe your style?

I have so many different styles that you could be excused for thinking I'm schizophrenic. The reason is that I love to immerse myself in a technique or style and then paint so many pictures until I've had enough and can't wait to try something new. That's why I have several collections. But there are two recurrent styles. One is concrete, naturalistic paintings and edited photographs, and the other is abstract paintings in strong colours and simple shapes.

On Instagram you add the hashtag #mindfulness. What's the connection between art and mindfulness?

The element that is common to all of my art is a certain serenity. I seek stillness in the process of painting and deliberately focus on the here and now. For me, this has something meditative. I think life has an essence of stillness, which is what I keep looking for. My intention is always to be thankful for who I am and what I have, including in my paintings. I think that's something you can see in the pictures.

Do you find this serenity on Sandhamn?

Definitely. There are no cars, just lots of nature. Sandhamn has been hyped up for a number of years now, and many rich people build villas, party and come for the summer months. But I still remember the island as a quiet, rural spot where everybody cycles everywhere and people shower in the garden. The crime author Viveca Sten was inspired by this transformation and the resulting clash between simple fishermen and snooty sailors in her Sandhamn Murders series.

Is there a place on Sandhamn visitors should definitely put on their list?

For me, the most beautiful publicly accessible spot is the Alexanderudden headland. It's beautifully wild and rocky. From there, you only see the open sea, no islands at all.

**www.alicemurray.se,
Instagram: @alicemurray**

Stockholm and its islands –
there's so much more to discover...

A YEAR IN STOCKHOLM

FESTIVALS AND EVENTS

FEBRUARY
Stockholm Design Week
This takes place in conjunction with the Stockholm Furniture Fair in early February, with parties, showrooms and events all over the city. Download the app for an overview.
www.stockholmdesignweek.com

APRIL
Kulturnatt
During this long night of culture, 150 museums, palaces, churches and galleries are open free of charge from 6 pm until midnight. Their programs are varied, and while there are often queues for attractions such as the opera house and royal palace, smaller venues are easier to get into.
www.kulturnattstockholm.se

APRIL/MAY
Cherry blossoms at Kungsträdgården
Taking a selfie under clouds of pink blossom in the royal gardens is a long-standing Stockholm tradition.

THROUGHOUT SUMMER
Grönan Live
Between May and September, the open-air stage in the Gröna Lund funpark hosts about 70 musicians, rock stars and pop bands. A 'green ticket' for entry to all concerts costs about 300 krona.
www.gronalund.com

JUNE
National holiday
The 6th of June is Sweden's national holiday. It is celebrated in honour of Gustav Vasa, who became king on 6th June 1523, when Sweden seceded from Denmark-dominated Kalmar Union. At the Skansen open-air museum and zoo, the event is honoured with traditional dances and a market. In the evening, the royal family travels from the palace to Skansen in horse-drawn carriages, attracting many onlookers.

Smaka på Stockholm

In early June, the Kungsträdgården park is transformed into a gourmet paradise where renowned chefs serve down-to-earth food in 40 food trucks and pop-up restaurants.

www.smakapastockholm.se

Midsummer

For many Swedes, celebrating the longest days of the year on the weekend closest to the 21st June is bigger than Christmas. A maypole is decorated and erected on the Friday (Midsummer's Eve), and people dance and enjoy traditional foods, such as herring, new potatoes, strawberry tarts and spirits. Locals party in the countryside, and in Stockholm there are public events, including in Skansen and Vinterviken park. For an authentic midsummer experience, go to an island in the archipelago such as Sandhamn, Utö, Vaxholm or Fjäderholmarna. Make sure you check the ferry timetables for your return trip or book accommodation in advance!

AUGUST

Kulturfestivalen & We Are Sthlm

In mid-August, a week of open-air cultural events welcomes Stockhomers back to the city from their holidays. The concerts, dance and theatre performances are free. The City Museum complements the performances by offering city walks on various themes. 'We Are Sthlm' is the festival program aimed at the younger generation.

www.kulturfestivalen.stockholm.se

AUGUST/ SEPTEMBER

Popaganda

This two-day festival with mostly Swedish pop musicians takes place at the Eriksdalsbadet public swimming pool.

www.popaganda.se

OCTOBER

Stockholm Jazz Festival

A whole week of 100 concerts at 20 venues – established in 1980, this festival is one of Sweden's oldest music events.

www.stockholmjazz.se

DECEMBER

Lucia

On 13th December, Sweden pays homage to Saint Lucy, the queen of light. Many churches, including Storkyrkan and St. Jacobs Kyrka, have moving candlelight concerts. *Lussebulle*, traditional yeasted St. Lucy's buns made with saffron, are served to sweeten the day.

www.svenskakyrkan.se/lucia

Christmas markets

During the dark winter, Stockholm transforms into a magical city with lavish lights across streets, lamps in windows and a number of Christmas markets. The epicentre of pre-Christmas joy is Stortorget square in the old town, closely followed by the festively decorated Skansen open-air museum. The traditional drink is *glögg*, served in small cups.

Julbord

In the weeks before Christmas, many families and work teams go out for dinner together. Restaurants offer special buffets with salmon and pickled herring, Christmas hams, hot dishes such as Jansson's temptation and desserts. Great places to go to include Södra Teatern, Brasseriet, Oaxen Slip, Fåfängan, Mr. French, Ulla Winbladh, Villa Godthem and Artipelag.

RECURRING EVENTS

SoFo Night

On the last Thursday of each month, stores stay open until 9 pm and invite shoppers in with specials, drinks and music.
www.sofo-stockholm.se

Fashion Week Stockholm

The latest autumn/winter fashion is showcased in January, and in late August the Stockholm runways give

you a glimpse of what's to come in the spring/summer season. Fashion Night makes for an excellent consolation for everyone who missed out on a ticket to the shows. Stores in Norrmalm and Östermalm are open late, and there are specials and latest designs on offer.
www.fashionweek.se
www.fashion-night.se.

Formex

At this design fair, held every January and August, 850 Scandinavian exhibitors showcase novelties and trends in home accessories, interior design and decoration.
www.formex.se

Designmarknad Sthlm

Every April, October and December, 60 designers and artists sell their works at the design market at the Färgfabriken arts venue.
www.designmarknadsthlm.se
www.fargfabriken.se

The long night of culture in April is a joint effort of 150 attractions and venues

PRATAR DU SVENSKA?

While Stockholmers will happily (and mostly quite fluently) speak English, you might want to try a few words in the local language. Swedish is friendly, resonant and not overly difficult, and Swedes like to keep things informal. If you need help or want to ask somebody something, try saying: **Kan du hjälpa mig?**

Swedish is a Germanic language, like English and German, and you'll probably have a good idea of what words mean simply by reading them. Listening and understanding is considerably more difficult, though, as Swedish has a few unique vowels, consonants and combinations of letters. The letter 'å' is pronounced as 'oh', 'y' as in 'mysterious', and a long 'o' as 'oo'. The letter 'g' is pronounced like the English 'y' in 'year' when it precedes 'e', 'i', 'ä' or 'y'.

Plus Swedish has a number of sibilant sounds, which are tricky for people not used to them and often don't sound anything like how they're spelled. The ending 'tion' is always pronounced 'shon', that is 'station' is pronounced 'stashon'. The letters 'k' and 'sk' are pronounced 'sh' if they precede 'e', 'i', 'ä' or 'y', and the combinations 'kj', 'tj', 'stj', 'skj' and 'sj' are pronounced as something in between 'sh' and 'kh'.

General expressions

Hi! – *Hej!* or *Hej hej!*
Bye! – *Hejdå!*
Take care! – *Ha det bra!*
Yes – *Ja*
No – *Nej*
Thank you – *Tack*
Excuse me – *Ursäkta*
May I ask you something? – *Får jag fråga dig?*
Where's…? – *Var ligger….?*
That's beautiful! – *Det är fint!*

Shopping

Where are the change rooms? – *Var finns omklädningsrummen?*
Do you have this in size S/M/L? – *Finns det här i storlek S/M/L?*
I'd like to pay please. – *Jag skulle vilja betala.*
Do you work here? – *Jobbar du här?*

I like this. – *Jag gillar det.*
Unfortunately it's too big/small. –
   Det är tyvärr för stort/för litet.
It's exactly right. – *Det är lagom.*
How much is it? – *Vad kostar det?*
That's too expensive for me. –
   Det är för dyrt för mig.
That's all, thanks. – *Det var allt, tack.*

Food & drinks
Breakfast – *frukost*
Lunch – *lunch*
Dinner – *middag*
Could we have a table for two/
   three/four please? –
   Vi skulle vilja ha ett bord för två/tre/
   fyra personer.
We'd like to sit outside. –
   Vi skulle vilja sitta ute.
This is delicious. – *Det smakar bra.*
Where are the toilets? –
   Var ligger toaletten?
I'd like … a cinnamon
   scroll. –
   Jag skulle vilja ha …
   en kanelbulle.
… meatballs. – *köttbullar*
… a sandwich. – *en smörgås*
   (*smørrebrød* is Danish!)
… a beer. – *en öl*
… a large beer (with over
   3.5% alcohol). – *en stor stark*
… a glass of white/red wine. –
   ett glas vitt/rött
Is the coffee topped up for free? –
   Är kaffet med påtår? (In most cafés,
   filter coffee is topped up for free
   as often as you like.)

The canal between Vasastan and Kungsholmen is shared by leisure boats, sightseeing boats and kayaks.

DIRECTORY

53 Clarion Hotel Sign
Östra Järnvägsgatan 35
Designer hotel; outdoor spa

20 COS
Biblioteksgatan 3
H&M sister store

184 Cultur
Österlånggatan 34
Gastropub

D
**188 Designfirman
Gamla Stan**
Västerlånggatan 40 & 68
Concept stores; home accessories

28 DesignTorget
Kungsgatan 52
Design products for the home

65 Downtown Camper
Brunkebergstorg 9
Hotel for active travellers

44 Drakenberg Sjölin
Hamngatan 11
Fine jewellery

152 Drop Coffee Roasters
Wollmar Yxkullsgatan 10
Coffee roasters & shop

96 Dusty Deco
Brahegatan 21
Furnishings store

E
43 Eataly
Biblioteksgatan 5
Gourmet meeting point

137 Eat With Jonna
Folkungatan 95
Light meals; smörrebrod creations

224 Erlands
Gästrikegatan 1
Cocktail bar

101 Ett Hem
Sköldungagatan 2
Exclusive boutique hotel

25 Eytys
Norrlandsgatan 22
Unisex shoes

F
120 Fablab
Bondegatan 7
Unique gift shop

39 Filippa K
Biblioteksgatan 2
Womenswear and menswear

154 Filippa K Second Hand
Hornsgatan 77
Second-hand fashion

162 Folkbaren
Hornsgatan 72
Bar next to the Folkoperan theatre

115 Fotografiska
Stadsgårdshamnen 22
Gallery: temporary exhibitions

237 Fryst
Kungsholms Strand 167
Popular ice-cream parlour

G
163 'Puckeln' gallery haven
Hornsgatan 26
Artist quarter

32 Generator
Torsgatan 10
Popular chain of hostels

145 Grandpa
Södermannagatan 21
Concept store: fashion & design products

H
246 Haga Tårtcompani & Bageri
Flemminggatan 107
Café

24 Hallwylska
Hamngatan 4
Bar: drinks & light meals, Sat. brunch

192 Lena M
Kindstugatan 14
Landscape paintings & vintage furniture

151 L'Homme Rouge
Krukmakargatan 29
Men's fashion

M

183 M17
Mälartorget 17
Café cum design shop

80 Malmstenbutiken
Strandvägen 5 B
Furniture, design classics

241 Mälarpaviljongen
Norr Mälarstrand 64
Dine in the garden or on the pontoon

113 Marimeko
Skånegatan 71
Finnish design: clothes & bags

126 Meatballs for the People
Nytorgsgatan 30
Rustic-cool restaurant

83 Mikkeller
Brahegatan 3
Microbrewery: bar with 24 kinds of draught beer

212 Mini Rodini
Odengatan 78
Childrenswear

191 Mister French
Skeppsbrokajen 103
Seafood restaurant

198 Moderna Museet
Exercisplan 4
Gallery for art from 1900

35 MOOD Stockholm
Regeringsgatan 48
Shopping centre: broad range of fashion & furnishings

168 Morfar Ginko
Swedenborgsgatan 13
Club, bistro, champagne bar

N

46 NK – Nordiska Kompaniet
Hamngatan 18–20
Art Nouveau palace with an exclusive ambience

161 Nitty Gritty
Krukmakargatan 24
Fashion haven for her & him

125 NOFO Hotel
Tjärhovsgatan 11
Hotel in SoFo

63 Nomad
Upplandsgatan 2
Restaurant with typically Swedish cuisine

50 Nosh and Chow
Norrlandsgatan 24
Stylish restaurant

90 Nordiska Galleriet
Nybrogatan 11
Established design haven

236 Norrmälarstrands Blommor
Norr Mälarstrand 30
Florist

41 Nygårdsanna
Mäster Samuelsgatan 6
Comfortable clothes

O

129 OAS
Åsögatan 28
Swimwear

140 Omayma
Skånegatan 92
All-day breakfast

243 Orangeriet
Norr Mälarstrand 464
Bar on the promenade

92 Oskar & Clothilde
Birger Jarlsgatan 27
Curios

93 Östermalms Saluhall
Östermalmstorg
Gourmet market hall

AUTHOR AND PHOTOGRAPHER

Lisa Arnold graduated in German and Scandinavian studies and has lived in Stockholm since 2013. She writes travel guides about Scandinavian destinations and reports on current and cultural affairs in northern Europe as a foreign correspondent for the *Wiener Zeitung* newspaper.

Shaped by water: the fascinating island city of Stockholm.

Published in 2020 by Murdoch Books, an imprint of Allen & Unwin

First published in 2019
© 2019 NG Buchverlag GmbH
Licensee of National Geographic Partners, LLC. © 2019 National Geographic Partners, LLC.

Murdoch Books Australia
83 Alexander Street
Crows Nest NSW 2065
Phone: +61 (0) 2 8425 0100
murdochbooks.com.au
info@murdochbooks.com.au

Murdoch Books UK
Ormond House, 26–27 Boswell Street
London WC1N 3JZ
Phone: +44 (0) 20 8785 5995
murdochbooks.co.uk
info@murdochbooks.co.uk

For corporate orders & custom publishing, contact our business development team at salesenquiries@murdochbooks.com.au

Responsible: Annika Wachter, Ulrich Jahn
Editor: Helga Peterz
Sub-editor: Anke Höhne
Internal design: Elke Mader
Cartography: Kartographie Huber, Heike Block
Prepress: LUDWIG:media

Publisher: Corinne Roberts
Translator: Claudia McQuillan
English-language editor: Ariane Durkin
Cover design: Jackie Richards
Production director: Lou Playfair

Photo credits: All photos in the body of the book and on the cover are by Lisa Arnold, except: p. 5: unsplash.com p. 29 under & other stories; p. 30 top left and p. 31 bottom: Susanna Blåvarg; p. 32 (all): Måns Berg Photography AB; p. 33: Acne Studios; p. 45 top: Foto TAK; p. 45 bottom: Charlie Drevstam 2017; p. 45 centre left: Magnus Skoglöf; p. 45 centre right: Anton Renborg; pp. 50, 57 (all): Mathias Nordgren; p. 51: Wolfgang Kleinschmidt; p. 53 bottom: Jonas Borg; pp. 60/61 (all): HOBO; pp. 64, 65, 196 (all): Erik Nissen Johansen; p. 66: Camilla Lindqvist; p. 102: Gastrologik; p. 115 top: Fredrik Rollmann; p. 125 (all): Hotel NOFO; p. 194 left and top right: Martin Botvidsson; p. 194 bottom: Stefan van der Kwast Gissberg; p. 198 bottom and top left, p. 203 top: Åsa Lundén/Moderna Museet; p. 200: Andrea Björsell; p. 203 bottom: Östling, Matti; p. 226: Jonatan Lastbom; p. 247 (all): Amaranten; p. 248: Nyréns. p. 274 and p. 277: unsplash.com.

ISBN 978 1 76052 583 5 Australia
ISBN 978 1 91163 291 7 UK

NATIONAL LIBRARY OF AUSTRALIA

A catalogue record for this book is available from the National Library of Australia

A catalogue record for this book is available from the British Library

Printed by C & C Offset Printing Co. Ltd., China

MIX
Paper from responsible sources
FSC
www.fsc.org   FSC® C008047